Unlocking Life's Secrets:

An Exploration of BodyMindSpirit

George W. Barnard M.D.

All rights reserved. No part of this book shall be reproduced or transmitted in any form or by any means, electronic, mechanical, magnetic, photographic including photocopying, recording or by any information storage and retrieval system, without prior written permission of the publisher. No patent liability is assumed with respect to the use of the information contained herein. Although every precaution has been taken in the preparation of this book, the publisher and author assume no responsibility for errors or omissions. Neither is any liability assumed for damages resulting from the use of the information contained herein.

Copyright © 2015 by George W. Barnard M.D.

ISBN 978-1-4958-0942-2 Paperback
ISBN 978-1-4958-0943-9 eBook

The information in this book is intended for educational and spiritual purposes only. It is not intended for the contents of this book to be used as a diagnostic/therapeutic instrument for physical, mental, or emotional problems. If the reader is not certain if he/she has a sufficient degree of mental or emotional stability to process the material in this book, he/she should first consult with his/her physician, therapist, or counselor. This book should not be considered a substitute for medical or therapeutic advice, diagnosis, or treatment. Any use of or reliance on any information contained in this book is solely at the reader's own risk. The author of "Unlocking Life's Secrets: An Exploration of BodyMindSpirit" assumes no liability for the material contained in this book or for the reader's actions or responses to the material contained in the book.

Please note that all of the names of patients used in this book are fictional.

∞

INFINITY PUBLISHING
1094 New DeHaven Street, Suite 100
West Conshohocken, PA 19428-2713
Toll-free (877) BUY BOOK
Local Phone (610) 941-9999
Fax (610) 941-9959
Info@buybooksontheweb.com
www.buybooksontheweb.com

Jan 14, 2016

To our friend Tom — who shows
his love in so many ways.
　　　Enjoy the book
　　　　　　George

Table of Contents

Dedication XIII
Appreciation XIV
Introduction XV

Chapter 1: Multi-Dimensional Self 1
  Many Faceted Self 1
  Watching the Mind 3
  Experiencing My Essential Nature 4
  Inner Resources 6
  Letting Be 7
  Judgmental Self 8
  Changing My Response to Criticism 13
  Reclaiming My Wholeness 17
  Experiencing the Freshness of My Being 18
  Genuine Concern for the Other 19
  Becoming We-centric 21
  Encountering the Divine 28
  Finding God/dess Within 30
  Harnessing Primordial Energies 33
  Liberation from Resentment and Hatred 36
  Lovers Loving 40
  Emerging from an Act of Betrayal 43
  'Tis a Gift 48

Chapter 2: Finding Secrets Within 49
  A Secret No More 49
  Seeking an Anchor 51
  Expanding My Boundaries 54
  Birthing the Stone 55
  Encouraging Him On 57
  Experiencing Being 59
  Finding a Safe Haven 60
  Having Self-Compassion 63
  Inward Bound 66
  Experiencing the Numinous 70
  Journey of Change 71
  Kundalini 73
  Path to Freedom 74

Chapter 3: Suffering and Healing 76
  Approaching Retirement 76
  Walking from the Cave of Darkness 78
  Connection to the Primal 79
  Sharing Life's Breath 80
  Inner Transformation 81
  Mythic Journey 82
  Prisoner in My Own Being 86
  Lifting the Veil from Childhood Emotions 88
  Moving On 93
  Entering My Sacred Space 95

Forgiveness Is Mine	98
Gaining Access to Healing Memories	100
I Ask Your Forgiveness	103
Letting Go of Old Tapes	104
Maitri	106
Miracles Still Happen	108
My Heart Grew Hands	109
Conquering Fear	110
My Spiritual Gourd	114
Reply from the Thou	116
The Perfect Hostess	117
Seeking the Watering Hole	120
Suffering Is Part of Isness	122
The Inner Crucible	124
Longing for a Life that Matters	126
The Re-Awakening	128
The Aftermath of Sexual Assault	137
Unfolding From Being	143
Unnamed Woman	144
You Are Accepted	147
Who Benefits from Forgiveness?	150
Homecoming	152
With Forgiveness Comes Relief	153

Chapter 4: Link to the Divine ... 155
Chit-Sat-Ananda/Awareness-Being-Bliss ... 155
essence is Essence ... 158
Feast at the Master's Table ... 159
Finding Harmony in the Numinous ... 161
Getting Through to God ... 163
Giving Up My Blindness ... 164
God Needs Me ... 165
I – As Co-Creator ... 166
Joyful Reunion ... 167
Life Sparks ... 168
Finding the One ... 169
Motion of the Butterfly ... 170
Realizing God's Presence ... 171
Say Hello to God ... 175
Spirit Waiting for Me ... 176
The Empty Vessel that is Full ... 177
True Identity ... 178
Loosen My Bond ... 179
With Spirits Renewed ... 180
You Are Not Alone ... 181

Chapter 5: Brain and Evolution ... 183
Being Human ... 183
One Integrated Brain ... 187
Old and New Responses to Threat ... 192

Secrets of the Brain 195
Evolutionary Brain 199
Humans Become Social Beings 204
How Our BodyMindSpirit Communicates 210
Perils of the Danger-O-Stat 217
Getting in Harmony with the Eternal 222
Experiencing the Power of the Amygdala 224
The Wonders of Oxytocin 229
Unlocking One of Life's Secrets 232
Learning Self-Regulation 235
Bonding Behavior 239

Chapter 6: Stress 242
The Overstressed Mom 242
Member of the Club 246
Coping with Stress 251
The Dynamics of Stress 254
Learning to Let Go of Chronic Stress 260
Preventing an Emotional Meltdown 264
Stress Burnout 267
Sympathetic Nervous System Overload 269
Post-traumatic Stress Disorder (PTSD) 272

Chapter 7: Relationships 276
Attunement 276
Complicated Families 280

Early Traumatic Relationships Impact Us 282
Facing a Big Decision..285
Getting Closure through Acceptance 288
Him and His Old Dog..290
Laboring to Bring Forth a New Creation.....................292
Letting Go 294
Mammy 297
Midwife – Guide – Mentor 298
Moments to Cherish 300
Now I am the Gardener...301
Our Home is Special 303
Welcome Home My Son..304
Receiving The Bouquet...307
Seeking and Receiving Blessings 308
Spring Ecstasy 309
Standing on the Shoulders 311
Endorphin Bursting Into Glee 313
In My Footsteps 314
Unfolding Into Wholeness 317
A Stranger No More 318

Chapter 8: Living a Full Life..319
A Model of Love 319
Enjoying the Joy 321
Fears from Childhood 322
Accepting Nurturance from the Soul...........................323

How Memories Influence Us 324
Becoming Aware of Love 327
Hungry for the Beloved 328
Let Us Open Our Hearts 329
She Still Has the Memory 330
The Power of Compassion 331
The Origins of Love 333
Two Basic Needs 337
The Power of the Heart 338
Gratitude 339
Gestation of the Love Child 340

Chapter 9: Death 342
The Final Letting Go 342
Dealing with My Mortality 343
Facing Death Without Fear 344
Goodbye Dear Friend 346
I Knew Him So Well 347
The Aftermath of Death 348
Sweet Words Lingered On 350
Journey Called Mourning 351
Goodbye Friend – Hello Angel 352
Learning to Befriend Death 353
Lessons of Life/Death 355
Life and Death as Process 357
Her Friend Helen 359

On Dying 360
One Drop of Water 361
Surrendering to Death 362
The Rosebud 364

Bibliography 366
Index of Poems 391

Dedication

I am extremely pleased to dedicate this book to Pat, my wife of more than 63 years. Throughout all of these years, Pat has been a constant source of love and support for me. Her unwavering love has not only assisted me in learning about love, it has also helped me in my emotional and spiritual growth process. I am extremely grateful to Pat for all of her loving traits.

Appreciation

This book could not have come to fruition without the wonderful assistance of our daughter, Brenda Birdsall. I greatly appreciate all that she has done. I also want to give my thanks to her husband, Bruce, who read the manuscript and made many helpful comments.

The beautiful art work on the cover of the book was done by my good friend and fellow psychiatrist, Robert Blakey, M. D.

I want to give special thanks to all five of our children and their spouses: Bill and Sandi, David and Sonoko, Beth and Bob, Brenda and Bruce, and Julie and John, for their ongoing love and friendship through all of our time together. I also want to extend love to our grandchildren Alex, William, John Russell, Lauren, Christina, and Maya, and to our great grandchild Reed.

Introduction

The content of this book has been created over a period of thirteen years. The book contains 156 poems – or reflections – on different topics related to the BodyMindSpirit (In order to emphasize the unity of the body, mind, and spirit, I have combined the three words into one word). Each poem reflects an issue that I was contemplating that day. Some days my contemplation process just seemed to flow by itself and at other times it was a challenging task. As you will see, many poems address the same issue from different perspectives.

Chapter 1 – Multi-Dimensional Self

These poems address the essential question "Who am I?" Most of us only identify with our Ego. We think that we are only our personality and our drives to experience pleasure and avoid pain. The Ego is helpful from the standpoint of the survival of the species, however it limits our ability to experience our own wholeness. In reality, we are a lot more complex than a one dimensional Ego. Indeed, we are a multi-dimensional Self, and Ego or Ego-Self is only one small component of our Authentic or Total Self.

In this chapter, you are introduced to different aspects of the multi-dimensional Self, including the Child Self, the Shadow Self, the Judgmental Self, the Ego Self, the Observer-Witness Self, and the Divine

Self. These different dimensions of ourselves, when combined, constitute the **Authentic or Total Self**. Since you may not be familiar with these different concepts, I'll take this opportunity to introduce you to the terms, so that as you encounter them, you will have a better understanding of their meaning.

The **Child Self** is that part of ourselves that carries some of the negative effects of the trauma that we experienced in childhood into the present moment. This trauma has basically wounded us, so that we see the present reality through the eyes of a child that has experienced great pain. The trauma has created non-conscious, implicit memories and reactions in our mind and body that can be triggered and threatened by current external or internal stimuli.

The **Judgmental Self** will cause us much grief. The Judgmental Self is a part of the **Shadow Self** – that part of ourselves that we do not want to own or accept. Judgmental Self is that part of our being that wants to find fault with who we are and with what we are doing. It is a blamer and makes us feel bad about ourselves.

The **Ego Self** is that part of ourselves which is almost exclusively preoccupied with obtaining pleasure and avoiding pain. The Ego Self is solely concerned with its own selfish desires and wishes. The Ego Self primarily identifies itself with our personality.

When we function as **Observer-Witness Self**, we are functioning at a higher level of being than Ego. As Observer-Witness Self, we have a more objective view of what is taking place in our lives than when we function as Ego. This is because Observer-Witness Self is more detached than Ego and therefore can consider interests other than its own.

Another component of our Authentic or Total Self is **Divine Self**. This dimension of our being operates from a higher state of being than both Ego and Observer-Witness Self. When we are able to function as Divine Self, we are able to act from a selfless perspective, such as showing compassion and forgiveness, which we cannot do when we function as Ego.

Fortunately, to some degree, we have a choice. We can choose whether we function from a lower state of being or from a higher, more integrated state of being.

First, we need to know that these various levels exist. Next, we have to meet and overcome the resistances that Ego will put up to prevent us from experiencing these higher states of being.

We can be thankful that we can call on our internal allies, Observer-Witness Self and Divine Self, to assist us in our encounters with Judgmental Self, Shadow Self, and Ego Self. Observer-Witness Self can provide support by assisting us to become aware of false but destructive beliefs that we have

XVII

brought with us from childhood. Divine Self can lend us nurturance through its love and compassion.

Throughout the book you will encounter poems addressing the many different components of our Authentic or Total Self. With practice, we can help our experience of Observer-Witness Self and Divine Self evolve from temporary states into more enduring traits. It requires strong determination and persistence to move to a higher state of being, and it is most certainly worth the effort.

Chapter 2 – Finding Secrets Within

In this chapter, you will discover that our reality may not be what we were taught as children. You will learn that there is both a material reality and a reality of the Divine Spirit. This reality of the Divine Spirit can be accessed by leaving our ordinary mode of being and entering a Meditative State.

While this Meditative State can be accessed in different ways, the one I describe most frequently in my poems is focusing on my breath and relaxing my body. Once I am relaxed, I then use imagination and visualization to experience a higher state of being. Since on one level our brain does not differentiate between our imagination and a real experience, we can use our imagination and creativity to bring about desired states of being.

In this Meditative State, I relive times from the past and, as Observer-Witness Self, I view myself as I was then, and others as they were then. Simultaneously, I observe myself as I am now.

While in this Meditative State, I am able to communicate with my imaginative mind and ask that I relive experiences from my past, but function from a higher state of being than I was able to do earlier. This process lays down new, more adaptive ways of functioning and new neuronal paths that aid in the effort to live from a higher state of being.

Chapter 3 – Suffering and Healing

In this chapter, we see again and again that suffering is here to stay. Each of us will have many occasions to experience suffering and become aware of how we approach this very complex issue. Whether we like it or not, suffering will be with us and it will give us many opportunities to get to know ourselves a little better.

While we cannot escape suffering altogether, we can learn to deal with it more effectively than we have in the past. We certainly can learn to have compassion for ourselves as well as forgiveness for those who have wronged us. We can also have forgiveness for ourselves when we have brought suffering to others and/or ourselves. Throughout it all, it becomes clear that we do a much better job of forgiving when we are able to function as Divine Self rather than as Ego.

In this chapter I have included several case histories of patients I have treated so that it becomes clear that, even in very severe cases, there is hope for recovery and opportunity to experience happiness. If we are to become free from suffering, we must be willing to change. We must be willing to let go of previous ways of functioning and apply newly-learned ways of being. Our letting go can be experienced as a form of death and resurrection in spiritual terms or as neuroplasticity in neuroscience terms. Either way, it will take courage to face the unknown and willingness on our part to be different than we have been. This transformation involves us forming an intent and then practice-practice-practice. This process also calls for a tremendous amount of self-forgiveness.

Chapter 4 – Link to the Divine

In today's technologically-oriented world, many people find it difficult to believe that anything besides the material world exists. And yet there are others who reject this belief and state that if only we open our hearts, we can actually experience the Divinity that exists all around us. I count myself in the latter group.

But I must admit to you that it has not been easy for me to reach this point. I believe this is because I have been so Ego-dominated and, as we know, Ego does not wish to accept that there are higher powers or forces than itself. In order to see the early poems reflecting this painful process, I invite you to read my book "In Search of Soul: Journey Toward Wholeness." The process of my spiritual unfoldment continues to be revealed in "Unlocking Life's Secrets: An Exploration of BodyMindSpirit."

The poems in Chapter 4 reflect the painful fact that learning to let go of the Ego-centric barriers that keep us from experiencing God's love is not simple. On this spiritual journey we find that we are constantly putting up resistances, due to the Ego's fear of the unknown. Our task becomes much easier if we can make contact with our inner powers that function from higher states of being than Ego, namely Observer-Witness Self and Divine Self. We can choose to let them be our primary inner guides rather than Ego. These guides dwell within us and can make our lives a lot less stressful if we can learn to depend on them.

As we are able to believe in the existence of Observer-Witness Self and Divine Self, and feel safe in trusting them, it becomes easier for us to open ourselves even more. This process of trusting and becoming more open allows us to experience the Divine Spirit (God) dwelling within us. Once we experience God's unconditional love for us, our healing process is hastened and it becomes easier and easier to find true harmony in our lives.

Chapter 5 – Brain and Evolution

Many of us do not realize how long it has taken the present day brain (along with the rest of the body) to evolve to its present form. It has taken millions of years, with many changes along the way, for our human brain to evolve to the point it is today. In many ways we could say that our brain is an evolutionary brain.

Louis Cozolino, in his book, "The NeuroScience of Psychotherapy: Healing the Social Brain," explains how the more modern components of the brain, called the cortical system, permit us to consciously make decisions. However, the more ancient components of the brain, called the sub-cortical system, make the majority of decisions at a non-conscious level, i.e., out of our awareness.

Stephen Porges, in his book "The Polyvagal Theory: Neurophysiological Foundations of Emotions, Attachment, Communication and Self-Regulation," explains in great detail how, from an evolutionary standpoint, the ancient, non-conscious components of the brain make crucial decisions without our awareness. For example, when we meet a person we non-consciously decide whether or not the person is a threat to us.

If we want to influence or modify the decisions made on the non-conscious level, we need to learn how to communicate with both the modern and ancient components of the brain. Since there is a two-way communication system between the modern and ancient components of the brain, they can influence each other and determine which will be more dominant in any particular moment.

Similarly, on a broader scale, the body and brain are an intricate, unified system, and there is constant two-way communication between the components of bodybrain. (I refer to it as bodybrain to reflect that it is one unit, as is BodyMindSpirit.)

All forms of psychotherapy demand that we gain access to this very complex communication system. While we have a long way to go, we are beginning to understand how the bodybrain communication system functions. This chapter reveals some of the insights gained in recent decades.

Chapter 6 – Stress

The research of Sonia Lupien, in her book "Well Stressed: Manage Stress Before It Turns Toxic," has shown that there are four factors that lead to stress: novelty, the unexpected, threat to the Ego, and the sense of not being in control. The poems in this chapter reflect my understanding of these four factors that lead to stress and what we can do to alleviate or prevent chronic stress.

In this chapter I also discuss the findings of Kerstin Moberg and Roberta Francis in their book "The Oxytocin Factor: Tapping the Hormone of Calm, Love and Healing." We not only have a Threat-Challenge-Defense System that produces the stress hormones Adrenaline and Cortisol, but we also have a Calm-Connection System that produces the anti-stress hormone Oxytocin.

Since one of the major factors that produces stress is some form of threat to Ego, then if we are to learn means of decreasing our stress, we must learn to function from a higher state of being than Ego. This involves us making the transition to function as Observer-Witness Self and Divine Self. In addition, we can learn other self-regulatory techniques that will aid us in the process of lowering our levels of stress.

Chapter 7 – Relationships

The poems in this chapter are taken from real life experiences and reflect both the sweetness and the pain experienced in relationships.

The poems address how the way we interact with others as adults is highly conditioned and determined by the initial bonding that we have with our mothers/caretakers. This initial relationship creates an imprint that determines our basic trust/distrust of the world and of people.

Through this mother/child bonding process we also learn how to regulate/control our body processes and behavior. As a young infant we cannot fulfill our own basic needs and therefore we learn to communicate our needs to our mother/caretaker non-verbally. All of our subsequent relationships are influenced by this early bonding process which has a profound influence on our lives.

Chapter 8 – Living a Full Life

Psychophysiological research has often been faulted for dealing primarily with the "negative" emotions such as fear, anger, anxiety, depression, guilt, and shame, and ignoring the "positive" emotions of joy, compassion, love, gratitude, and acceptance. The poems in this chapter deal with both the positive and negative emotions that we experience in everyday life.

Many of the poems in this chapter specifically address the issue of defensiveness, and how it not only negatively affects the way we relate with people but also the way we relate to the Divine. This resistance to open our hearts and share our vulnerability with others prevents us from being able to experience love and compassion. The poems in this chapter offer some practical approaches for how to become less defensive and develop the ability to show compassion to ourselves and others.

Chapter 9 – Death

I am sure many of you are wondering why I – or anyone – would want to include a chapter on death in a book of poems. When I was nine years old, I was traumatized by my father's death, and I am still wrestling with death and its meaning for me. (For any of you that want to learn more about my painful process in dealing with my father's death, you can read my book "In Search of Soul: Journey Toward Wholeness.") For those of you who may have also been traumatized by the death of a loved one, I want to offer you hope. Although I have not fully recovered from the death of my father, I have made significant progress in the healing process.

I am now 87 years old and it seems as though I lose a relative or friend every week or two. These losses certainly make me aware that my own death is not too far away. I am curious as to how I will deal with that final "letting go."

As you read the poems in this chapter, understand that they were generated from my own experience. As I approach my own death, I realize that I am not alone because Divine Spirit and my other inner allies are with me. I also believe that I have nothing to fear. I have had a full life and I believe that after I die I will continue to exist in some Spirit form. As the rivers merge with the ocean, so I will merge with Consciousness and continue to exist.

Suggestions for the Reader

As you can see, the poetry in this book is free-flowing and does not include commas or periods. The reason for this approach is so that you can experience the poems more as oral, rather than written, speech. More importantly, I would like for the poems to activate both the right and left hemisphere of your brain, so that your reading is both an intellectual and emotional experience.

Take your time as you read through the book.

You may decide to sample poems from various chapters and see which ones resonate for you on that particular day.

Read one or two poems and then "chew on them" so you can see how, if at all, the poems may be speaking to you about a current issue in your life.

Read some portions silently and other portions aloud so that you approach the content from different perspectives and use different senses.

Most importantly, I hope that you enjoy the experience of reading this book.

Chapter 1: Multi-Dimensional Self

Many Faceted Self

*When I experience myself
as worthy – precious – valuable
I will honor myself*

*When I experience myself
as strong – powerful – energetic – efficient
I will respect myself*

*When I experience myself
as vulnerable – needy – fragile
I will be gentle with – befriend myself*

*When I experience myself
as hungry – in pain – cold
I will nurture – relieve – protect myself*

*When I am tense – worried – anxious – frightened
I will relax – calm – reassure myself*

*When I am angry – enraged
even then I will respect myself –
I can be the nonjudgmental observer –
accept myself – explore myself –
find what is beneath the furor*

*Have I discovered yet that I am a
many faceted – many dimensional creature
I need to know all facets of this diamond*

*I need to be patient – let all my characters be
I am both my master and my slave –
my tormentor and my savior –
Each aspect of me has a meaning – a purpose*

*I need to be curious – be receptive –
seek to understand my multi-dimensional Self*

*Herein is my holy place
Herein is my wholeness*

∞

George W. Barnard M.D.

Watching the Mind

*If I watch my mind in action
it flits from subject to subject like a bee
tasting first this flower and then that one*

*The mind is most often restless
and has difficulty remaining quiet and still*

*In watching the mind I can
identify myself as the watcher or the watchee*

*As the watchee I feel strung out –
in disharmony – hurried and chaotic*

*If I identify myself as the watcher
I experience quietness and calmness*

*As the watcher I am more centered and in balance
I switch from the doing mode to the being mode*

I am detached from the whirlwind about me

I am Observer-Witness Self

∞

Experiencing My Essential Nature

*Do I really know the essential nature of who I am
Am I able to experience the essential me*

*I can't if I am forever projecting onto the Other
Whether I am projecting my
good qualities onto the Christ
or projecting my bad qualities
onto the Anti-Christ
In either case I am alienated from an essential part of me
A part I disown – I disclaim*

*It is only when I withdraw these projections –
and then reclaim – re-own them –
that I come to experience my essential nature*

*To do this takes courage –
courage both to let go – and courage to accept*

*Courage to let go of my striving for
moral perfection – my Ideal Self
And courage to accept my imperfect being
as I am – my Total Self*

*My courage to let go is a form of death
I must let go of a cherished part of who
I thought I could become*

*My courage to accept is a form of
resurrection – of rebirth*

George W. Barnard M.D.

As I forgive myself – I am redeemed into a new life
This acceptance of my imperfection
gives me great flexibility

I can think evil – I can feel evil –
without doing evil – without being evil

This keeps the tension between good and evil
within me – where I have more control

If I leave my evil thoughts in my unconscious
I am more likely to project them onto the Other –
since I am unable to accept them as part of me

When the tension between good and evil
is in balance within me
then I am in balance

∞

Inner Resources

He is forever within me
The one I call
Guide – Friend – Warrior – Mentor
Sophia – Companion – Compassion

Wherever I am on my journey
Guide is always there

If in despair Friend gives me comfort
when I am afraid of falling into the abyss

Warrior encourages me to make the leap
at those times when my defenses
want me to remain contracted

Mentor calls my hand – confronts me –
and reminds me I have a choice

If I am confused about a problem
or even lost along my way
Sophia is there with the wisdom
and guidance I need

During my moments of loneliness
Companion and I listen together in silence

And in my need for forgiveness
Compassion is ready
with an open heart
What resources they all are

∞

George W. Barnard M.D.

Letting Be

*My pain stayed with me through a long night
like a dull aching tooth
Wherever I went it was surely there
I had encountered my Shadow
and once again my Judgmental Self
was extracting its pound of flesh*

*I tried to run from my shame
but it would not allow me to escape
Then I decided to stay
and explore what this was all about*

*Why so much pain for simply having a dream
My unconscious had lowered its barrier
and allowed a part of me to be shown
that had not been revealed before*

*As my Observer-Witness Self I watched in detachment
as the shame went through its peaks and valleys
during the entire day*

*I simply remained with it – allowing it to be – trying to
get to know it for what it was and what it had to offer me
Then I realized that in my letting be – my acceptance –
I had transformed the non-acceptance
of the Judgmental Self*

*I further came to understand
that acceptance was healing grace
Oh the relief that comes with grace*

∞

Judgmental Self

*At times I have felt
incapacitated with guilt and shame*

*At times I have felt
overwhelmed with anxiety and fear*

*At times I have felt
burdened with a deep sense of failure*

*At times I have felt
tied up in knots of tension and worry*

*At times I have felt
super-critical of myself or others*

*At times I have felt
devastated by criticism that I received from others*

*As these situations applied to me
I looked behind them to see which powerful
but destructive force lurked within my psyche
Again and again I met my Judgmental Self*

*This too was a vigorous part of me –
When activated it functioned as an aspect of
my Shadow – so I learned to be on guard*

*Most often it was hidden from my awareness as it exerted
its harsh power as one of the unconscious forces
of rationalization – denial – projection*

George W. Barnard M.D.

*Even worse this super-critic had its origin
when I was a child – when I needed approval
from my parents – teachers – ministers –
so it is a deep part of me*

*It was from these authority figures that I learned
what was good – what was bad
But here is where the problem began*

*As a child I lacked the capacity to realize that
bad behavior does not equal a bad me
Unfortunately I identified with the voice that said
"You are bad"*

*In the deepest recesses of my mind
I developed the belief at my core that I was bad*

*As a result I felt unworthy – I lacked self-approval
This started me on my journey of striving for perfection*

*I did not know how to be gentle with myself
I did not know how to forgive myself
I did not know how to accept myself
I did not know how to honor myself –
how to respect myself*

*But all this turmoil lay hidden from my awareness
As I wore my Mask – my Pretend Self –
I convinced others – even myself –
that I was self-confident and capable
But underneath the Mask Self – a strong batch of
harshness – negativity – fermented*

Unlocking Life's Secrets

*From time to time I saw it erupt as volcanic rage –
or show itself in a more subtle way –
by being a workaholic or a non-feeling person
Harsh – judgmental – blaming attitudes
undermined the intimate relationships I had*

*My Judgmental Self is sneaky as well as tricky
so it is difficult to encounter directly*

*Most often I only see evidence that it has been there –
done its damage and moved on –
I am left with feelings I can't explain –*

*How then could I ever contact this elusive
force of negative – destructive energy*

*First to deal with the skepticism of my rational self
I had to put forth the idea that my Judgmental Self
existed – as a hypothesis to be tested
Then I began my search*

*On this journey to find and negotiate
with the elusive Judgmental Self
I needed to enlist the assistance of inner helpers –
my Observer-Witness Self – and my Divine Self*

*My Observer-Witness Self functions to keep me
detached and non-judgmental so I may more easily
give up my defenses and see things about myself which
I didn't want to see or else I have falsely believed
would be too painful to experience*

George W. Barnard M.D.

*My Observer-Witness Self provided me some protection
from the negative forces of my Judgmental Self*

*My Divine Self gave me the
nurturance and compassion that I needed
It also helped me learn self-forgiveness*

*My Divine Self functioned as my source of
wisdom and guidance as I engaged in
dialogue with my Judgmental Self
So that I may experience these inner parts of me
I have learned to carry out a ritual that allowed me
to gain entry to a Meditative State*

*I went deeply inside and made contact
with my unconscious Body Self –
so that the implicit became explicit
The body memories revealed themselves*

*As they did I remembered a time in my life
when I experienced a great amount of shame
after being criticized by a significant person in my life
This may have occurred a short time ago –
or it may have taken place during my childhood
I went back to that time of the memory I saw myself
as I was then – saw the other people as they were – noting
in particular their facial expressions
since this is where the truth lies*

*At the same time as I viewed myself as I was then
I allowed my Observer-Witness Self
to look on in a detached non-judgmental way*

Unlocking Life's Secrets

*I allowed this visual scene to become clear –
I allowed myself to feel as I did then –
to think as I did then –
to be able to hear what the other person was saying to me
I allowed myself to feel the shame –
feel it in my body as I did then
At the same time I allowed my Observer-Witness Self
to watch in a non-judgmental manner*

*Then – holding on to my remembering – re-experiencing
the shame – I became receptive to the acceptance –
the love – that my Divine Self was offering me*

*As I became aware of my goodness – my worthiness –
the undeserved feelings of shame melted away*

*I saw and heard the criticism in a different way
I experienced the criticism for what it could
honestly offer me as an adult – not for what it dishonestly
accused my Child-Self of being*

*I walked away with honor – with self-respect
With this experience I laid down
new neuronal tracts that in the future will
enable me to dialogue and negotiate
more easily with Judgmental Self*

Ah the joy that comes from neuronal plasticity

∞

George W. Barnard M.D.

Changing My Response to Criticism

*When I am criticized
I often feel hurt – wounded*

*If I am functioning as Child Self
it is hard to listen to what is being said*

*My hearing is deadened by emotional pain
so I become defensive and withdraw out of fear
or counterattack out of my old set of beliefs*

But I have options

*As Observer-Witness Self I can step aside
and experience the transactions with greater objectivity
I can listen to the criticism
without the degree of pain I have felt previously*

*As a child when I was criticized my Judgmental Self
deceived me to wrongly accept the beliefs
that my parents were always right
and I was always wrong
and that bad behavior equaled being a bad person*

*As a consequence I felt that I was being rejected
and seen as being unlovable
I carried these destructive beliefs with me into adulthood
Now I can change these beliefs*

As Observer-Witness Self
I will be able to listen to the criticism
without judging who is right and who is wrong –
without accepting the idea that I am an evil person –
without believing that I am unworthy of being loved

As Observer-Witness Self I can allow myself to be open –
and not to react out of fear – anger – guilt – shame

But if I should react in this destructive manner –
still I have the capacity to accept my
response with compassion

I will listen to the criticism not as a child –
but as an adult
Not believing I will be devastated – but informed

Nor must I accept automatically the
comments of the critic
Rather I will evaluate them
Then I will be patient and gentle with myself
as I practice – practice – practice

Let me remember – when I am being criticized
it is not the external critic who causes me emotional pain
but rather it is my internal Judgmental Self

This destructive – perfectionistic part of me is
what causes me to feel
guilty – shameful – unworthy – unloved

It is the negative component of me that calls forth
my explosive rage or my hasty withdrawal

*Both are expressions of my Sympathetic Nervous
System response to a perceived threat
Judgmental Self is also the function responsible for me
accepting undue blame and opening myself to
becoming a victim of abuse
It never offers me relief through forgiveness*

*The destructive forces of Judgmental Self
can be countered and balanced by the
creative healing energies of Divine Self that offer me
unconditional love and compassion
It provides the deep well of acceptance*

*Its positive forces keep me centered and focused
when I am receiving the wrath of another
It holds me in balance so I neither
counterattack or run away in fear*

*And when I falter or do a wrong –
Divine Self provides the grace of self-forgiveness and
dissipates the negative and destructive
feelings of guilt and shame*

*Often Divine Self lies hidden from my awareness
because of my denial – distrust – defensiveness*

*It is vital to my well-being that I seek to find –
uncover – befriend Divine Self
And then enhance its ability to unfold and blossom*

If successful then when I am being criticized I will:

Take several deep breaths
Turn inward
Enter a Meditative State
Contact Divine Self
Seek its wisdom and guidance
Ask for its assistance
to rebalance the internal warring forces
and thereby decrease the power of Judgmental Self

I will seek to be receptive to the nurturance
and support provided by Divine Self
I will give it permission to act on my behalf

I do not deny the power of Judgmental Self
but even more essential I realize – honor – respect
the power of Divine Self

It has the ability to converse with the Judgmental Self
and through creative dialogue is able to cancel out the
destructive power of the Judgmental Self
and also is able to heal the wounds Judgmental Self
has caused to my Soul and my Spirit

∞

George W. Barnard M.D.

Reclaiming My Wholeness

*I can truly experience
my genuineness – my authenticity:*

*when I shed my Mask – my pretend Self –
that part of me that is false*

*when I drop my arrogance – pride –
all markers of the self-will of Ego –*

*when I claim ownership of my Shadow –
those unacceptable parts of me which were put away –*

when I tone down the harshness of Judgmental Self –

*when I learn the skills and wisdom of
Observer-Witness Self –*

*when I discover the marvelous riches
within the Divine Self –*

*when I open my heart and become
receptive to receive love
and guidance from the Divine Spirit –*

*when I use these as roadmaps
to heal my woundedness
to reclaim my wholeness*

*Did I say all this takes
practice – patience – persistence*

∞

Experiencing the Freshness of My Being

*If I am to find meaning to life
If I am to be healed – to become whole –
I must learn to be receptive –
to surrender my will*

*I must allow – yes – even invite –
the unconscious to become conscious
I must subjugate the Ego to the Self*

I do this through my dreams – my imagination

*I simply permit myself to become aware –
to lower my defenses and resistances
to that marvelous creative reservoir –
the unconscious*

*I must drop my know-it-all attitude
about who I am – or might become*

*I begin to welcome my opportunity
to strip away the Mask – the fake me –
and experience the freshness of my being
as the spring welcomes the daffodil*

*The daffodil in turn experiences its wholeness
as it peaks its head out of the snow
and accepts itself as the mystery of being –
as the glory of spring*

∞

George W. Barnard M.D.

Genuine Concern for the Other

*Can I ever get beyond my own concerns
and be genuinely concerned for the Other*

*If I am to do this
I must undergo an inner transformation
and learn to integrate my neuronal circuits
on a higher state of functioning than at present*

*First I must lessen Ego's grip on me
in order to function as Divine Self*

*Once I know how to enhance the presence of
Divine Self within me then I can feel with the Other*

*As Divine Self I lower my tanka –
my desire for my own fulfillment –
for my own selfish cravings –
so that I can more fully be aware
of the needs of the Other
and fulfill the needs of the Other
without wanting anything in return*

*Instead of wanting to satisfy me –
fulfill my own desires –
as Divine Self I will want to satisfy the Other –
to do for the Other – to fulfill the needs of the Other*

*As Ego my seemingly bottomless pit of trishna –
my grasping desires – will never be filled*

*But as Divine Self I will be satisfied with – be content
with – a touch – a smile – from the Beloved
because I am able to empathize with the Other*

*But to function as Divine Self
Ego must be willing to bow its head – bend its knee –
and submit itself to the will of God/dess*

*If Ego can partially let go of its will
and share control with Divine Self
then I can live by the principle of Wu-Wei
the principle of letting be in which I obtain freedom
by aligning myself with the will of God/dess*

*To the extent that Ego can become receptive
to having its being changed by Being
and permit Divine Self to control my behavior
then my limited being becomes
linked with unlimited Being*

*It is then that I will be sustained by
life's higher integrative powers*

*From this harmonious relationship flows
wisdom – guidance – energy – calmness*

All indicators of high levels of neuronal balance

∞

George W. Barnard M.D.

Becoming We-centric

*There's one thing for certain about
being on a spiritual journey
Change is always present
Our inner world is never static*

*This principle especially holds true for
our different states of being*

*In different states we have an internal image
representation of who we are
For example most of us function a great
deal of the time as Ego*

*In this realm we are very Ego-centric
which basically means that we are
primarily concerned about ourselves*

*When I am functioning as Ego
I am primarily seeking that which gives me pleasure
and avoiding that which brings me pain*

*Being Ego-centric is best seen as being on a scale
and not as an all-or-none characteristic*

*When I am highly Ego-centric
I focus almost exclusively on me
and what I perceive as fulfilling my needs –
and there is little or no concern for the Other*

*If I move toward the other end of the scale
I begin to be more concerned about the needs of the Other
– or you could say I become less selfish*

*Our Ego-centricity begins in infancy
when we are entirely dependent on others
to meet our needs for survival*

*As infants we have many non-conscious functions
operating to aid us in meeting our needs for survival*

*For example when we are hungry but
cannot feed ourselves and
cannot verbally communicate our need for food –
still in some manner we must communicate our needs
non-verbally to our caretaker*

*To do this we may root for the nipple
or cry and signal that we are in distress*

*If our hunger signals are adequately received by our
caretaker and we are fed then our internal organs receive
the signal of the need having been met
This signal is then sent to the brain and
we have a feeling of satisfaction*

*Thus at a very early stage of life Ego-centricity begins
and continues through childhood and on
into later stages of development*

*By young adulthood our Ego-centric
approach is quite stable*

*Sometimes we are in a relationship with
another person that we care about
and we get little flits of being that are different than
our usual Ego-centric way of living*

*Suddenly we are experiencing a way of life
that is not Ego-centric but instead is We-centric
It is an I and Thou relationship*

*We discover that Ego is not the only
representative of who we are
Now the stage is being shared by Divine Self*

*This part of our being can consider
the needs of the Other*

Wow – we think – how can that be

*Although it may be fleeting we have experienced a
different reality*

*Hey - we think
I can be more than I thought*

*This brief moment is a state – a way of being
Not permanent but temporary*

*We think it is wonderful and we desire to
be there more frequently and stay longer –
to have State become Trait*

*This is moving our state of being to a higher state
for a longer time and on a more consistent basis*

But how

Basically to start is pretty simple
We begin with the intent – the desire –
and we set out to achieve that desired reality

But soon we encounter resistance – there is a barrier –
and we painfully learn that Ego
does not want to lose control
Ego wants – demands – that it be
the one and only one in charge

We all will meet resistance from Ego
as we make an attempt to function
from a higher state of being than Ego –
but each person's resistance
will show up in a different way

Let's say that a man is a problem drinker
This is just another way to say that he drinks to excess
but he denies it
Others can see it but he can't

He uses alcohol to escape from a painful reality –
one filled with suffering – fear – isolation – loneliness

But with alcohol briefly he is in a different reality

One that contains less pain – maybe even some joy –
but certainly more pleasant than the reality
he experiences when not drinking alcohol

*But one thing is certain
When his reality is dependent on alcohol
it is almost certain
that he is functioning from an Ego-centric base*

*Whether he likes it or not
Since he is a problem drinker
he is unable to consider the welfare of his loved ones
as much as he might like to do
Realizing this he sets out to change*

*It is at this point he forms the intent – the desire –
to function without alcohol*

*Essentially he is saying
"I am aware that functioning as Ego alone will not allow
me to achieve my desired goals*

*I need to move to
a higher state of being than Ego*

*I need to function daily from a state of being
that will permit me to consider the needs of the Other
as well as my own needs"*

*He doesn't have to kill Ego to accomplish this
He can simply broaden his concept of who he is
He is a multifaceted individual
when he is his Total Self
He will encounter some internal positive components that
enable him to accomplish more than he can
when he functions strictly as Ego*

*These positive components such as Observer-Witness Self
and Divine Self are his internal allies*

*He should also know that he will encounter some internal
negative components – such as
Judgmental Self – Shadow Self and Child Self –
that will cause him problems and he will need to
learn effective ways of dealing with them*

*The important thing for him to remember is
not to fear them or deny them
Instead he needs to treat them with respect and become
aware of what they have to teach him about himself*

*It is at this point he sets off on his spiritual journey
to meet both the allies and the enemies
The sooner he is able to take ownership of all the
characters he meets the better off he will be*

*He should greet each one and say "Howdy "
and then say to himself
"This too is part of me but I am more"*

*He can experience for himself all the wonderful things
that this diverse group of internal characters
and energies can bring to his life*

*For example functioning as Observer-Witness Self
enables him to step back and in a detached
non-judgmental mode look at himself while in action*

*As Observer-Witness Self he is more objective
because he is balancing several different
parts of the brain and in the process
is integrating thoughts and feelings*

*Functioning as Divine Self he is able to have
acceptance – compassion – and forgiveness for the Other
and seek to fulfill the needs of the Other*

*This is a new beginning for him
It will require time – practice – and patience*

But it is well worth the effort

∞

Encountering the Divine

How do I experience God

*First I empty my mind of conceptions –
of preconceptions – of what God may be*

*I become empty
empty of thoughts – empty of ideas
I become nothing
My self-importance disappears*

I move from being Ego-centric to being God-centric

*I become receptive –
willing to receive – willing to experience*

I finally realize the truth

*God is already within me
and can be experienced only
if I make the necessary inner changes*

*God will not coerce me into a relationship
God establishes a co-partnership through persuasion*

*I have freedom –
I have a choice whether or not to tune myself
to the inflow of the Divine –
to link myself in harmony
with the laws of the cosmic forces*

George W. Barnard M.D.

*Once I establish this bond with the Divine
I remain open to receive creative – rejuvenating – energy*

*I remain silent and listen to guidance
from the inner unseen source of Wisdom*

I remain receptive to receive love from the Beloved

*With this comes
calmness – equanimity – inner peace*

∞

Finding God/dess Within

*As a boy growing up
I was taught God was out there –
up there – in heaven*

*I was never taught
God is in here – in me*

*I was taught that this transcendental
God did become incarnate once in Jesus
But this still left God out there for me
I believed that was an absolute truth*

*But then I discovered it was only church doctrine –
a man-made belief – not a God-made truth*

In fact the doctrine had changed over time

*Between the fifth and thirteenth centuries –
following the arguments of Augustine –
Orthodox Christianity had preached
God exists within us*

*But then in the thirteenth century –
following the arguments of Aquinas –
the Church fathers declared
God exists outside us – as the Wholly Other*

This man-declared belief is still preached today

*I feel I have been deceived
I feel I have been cheated*

George W. Barnard M.D.

The very institution that claimed to teach me about God
in fact denied me the opportunity
to experience God/dess –
to experience God/dess within me

But on my own I decided
to find God/dess – to experience God/dess

It has been a struggle for me
I felt alienated
I thought I was unworthy
I found it hard to taste – to accept – Grace

Then I went within
to see – to experience – who I was –
not just my conscious being
but my unconscious being as well

And there I found Grace

There I found my connections –
not only with
my Shadow Self -
my Judgmental Self -
my Child-Self -
my Ego-Self - and
my Observer-Witness Self

But I also made connections with
my Divine Self and with
the Divine Spirit

*I allowed myself to relax – to hunker down –
to bask in the divine experience –
opening every cell of my Body
so the Divine could flow in and out
gently bathing my essence with sacred Essence*

*Bringing with it agape – unconditional love –
forgiveness – acceptance – of my imperfect but whole Self*

*Now I live with Grace –
wonderful Grace – marvelous Grace*

*Grace available for you –
Grace available for me*

∞

George W. Barnard M.D.

Harnessing Primordial Energies

*I need to face the fear of what I will find
if I look deep within myself*

*Let Ego have the courage – the strength –
both to explore and to be receptive
to the unconscious forces
as they emerge into consciousness*

*These primordial energies still exist within me –
influencing my thoughts – feelings – actions*

*These primordial forces communicate at a cellular level
with every aspect of my body
There is an interlocking of all the cells in my organism*

*As the unconscious primordial energy becomes conscious
it is conceptualized – perceived – experienced
as images – symbols – metaphors*

*Their meaning may not be readily apparent
nor can they be analyzed with logic*

*They must be approached with the intuitive mind
willing to permit disparate elements
to co-exist simultaneously*

*As I allow – accept – confront these previously
hidden – denied – functions/conflicts/complexes
to enter consciousness*

*I certainly will experience some suffering
Although I am afraid I go forward
I tell my conscious mind
that it will not be over-powered or overcome
by the unconscious energies*

*They are simply opposites of what I previously have been
willing to admit – to allow*

*Now I can permit the other pole into awareness –
thereby achieving psychic balance without coercion*

We all have these conflicts/complexes

*It is part of our spiritual journey to freedom
to allow these into awareness
and to suffer with the tension thereby created*

*This process will not destroy me
nor is it a sign of weakness or of illness
It is a part of the healing process*

*By bringing my conflicts/complexes
into my awareness –
by exploring them – allowing them to be –
without demanding that they go away
I thereby transform them*

*They no longer have their
negative – destructive hold on me
but their energy is now available for my use
in a positive – creative way*

George W. Barnard M.D.

Am I up to the task

I am if I don't try to do it solely as Ego

*I must move to higher states of being and function at times as Observer-Witness Self
and other times as Divine Self*

*And I certainly want to limit the actions of
Judgmental Self because of the negative influence
it brings with accusations – guilt – and shame*

∞

Liberation from Resentment and Hatred

*Many of us have been emotionally wounded
to some degree during infancy and childhood
And if not at that time then certainly in
adolescence and adulthood*

*After a while these little nicks and pricks begin to
take a toll on us and shape how we see life*

*One of the things that often happens to us is that when
we are emotionally wounded
we don't know how to let go of the pain*

*Too often we carry this pain around with us
in the form of resentment and hatred*

*These may sound like strong words and
I could change them a bit and
substitute the words bitter/cynical/pessimistic
if it makes you feel more comfortable*

*But the point is that too often
once we have been emotionally wounded
we just hold on and hold on to our suffering*

*In fact you could say that some of us
have become slaves to our suffering*

So how do we start the process of liberation

How do we learn to let go

*Well first if we look carefully at just
which part of us is suffering
we usually find that it is our Ego*

*Let us think back now and recall
when we were a teenager
and someone said something to us
that hurt our feelings*

*In other words our feelings of pride –
a hallmark of Ego – were deflated*

*We can move on a few years and now we are
on a complex job and feel that we don't have control of the
situation and our boss criticizes our work*

*Or we are married and our spouse
seems to find fault in everything we do
We begin to feel that we are of little value
We become more and more resentful toward our spouse
and the resentment seems to drain all the
love that we once felt for him/her
Gradually the space once occupied by love
is now filled with hatred and bitterness*

*But common to all of these stages is that we feel as though
Ego has been attacked and threatened*

*Now we are left with a burden of having these feelings
but not knowing how to let them go
At this point it is helpful to become aware that indeed
Ego is a part of who we are but we are more than Ego*

*We may not have discovered these parts yet
but they are there waiting for us to discover them*

*These other parts – such as our
Observer-Witness Self and our Divine Self –
offer us a way to freedom from our suffering –
or if not freedom –
certainly a great reduction in our suffering*

*But how can this be we ask
Because they will enable us to meet the challenges of life
with a lot more equanimity than can Ego*

Why is this so

*Because they operate on a higher state of being
or of brain integration than does Ego*

*To start they give us a different way of
viewing ourselves and our environment*

*They do not get as easily threatened as does Ego
Additionally when we are operating from these higher
states of being our Amygdala is not so easily activated
with an outpouring of the stress hormones –
Cortisol and Adrenaline*

*But I believe the most powerful thing that
Observer-Witness Self and Divine Self do for us is that
they provide us with the ability to have
love – compassion – and forgiveness
for ourselves
Ego just can't do this*

*Know that Observer-Witness Self and Divine Self
will protect us from the wrath and criticism of
Judgmental Self – a subsidiary of Ego*

*We can be aware of the Judgmental Self
finding fault in us
When this begins we can call on
the assistance of our helpers –
Observer-Witness Self and Divine Self*

*Functioning as these will allow us to negotiate with
Judgmental Self and bring us relief from harsh and undue
criticism and will also allow us to be kinder and more
accepting of ourselves*

*Functioning as these higher components of Self will allow
us to be loving – compassionate – forgiving – accepting
toward ourselves*

*And once this has an effect on us then we in turn
can be loving – compassionate – forgiving –
and accepting toward the Other*

∞

Lovers Loving

*I never knew until I experienced it
what a difference there is
between lovers loving as Ego
as compared with lovers loving as Self*

*When loving as Self –
each lover has been able to rid self
of his/her projection of the Other
and then become aware
of the uniqueness of the Other*

*To obtain this transpersonal stage of awareness
takes effort and is painful
But when suffering is embraced freely –
a new love being is born*

*In journeying from Ego-love to Self-love
each lover is able to a focus beyond his/her own needs –
to focus on the needs of the Other
Each lover is able to find his/her own separateness*

*Before the reunion can occur
each learns about his/her own inner forces – complexes*

*In order to break the automatic reactions
each becomes aware of behavior from the past
that shapes behavior in the present*

*Each unifies Ego with Self in order to find a higher love
in order to experience the flow of love from the universe
as it flows into and through their being*

*Ego-love to a large degree is identified with
the collective Other – with Persona
whereas Self-love has discarded identification with
Masked Self and has a broadened identification
to include Shadow and other aspects of the unconscious*

*Self-love becomes aware of its uniqueness
and differentiation from the collective core*

*When in Self-love lovers connect on
a new plane of reality – the plane of the divine –
the plane of Divine Spirit*

*It is here the divine of yang
mingles with the divine of yin
There is mystery – magic – enchantment
Life has its wet – potent energy of the deep instincts
Raw energy of yang mixes with raw energy of yin*

*God passion connects with Goddess passion
Pure demonic power wherein lovers are possessed
Time is suspended as
primordial intertwines with primordial
Each partner transcends ordinary reality
as Soul reflection mirrors Soul reflection*

*Here there is no personal identity
but a beckoning of cosmos to cosmos*

*Renewed and renewing –
each emerges once again into the world of ordinary being
Each now aware of his/her own eros being –
a being of love – a being of relationship*

Unlocking Life's Secrets

*Having tasted the world of yin/yang energy
they are comfortable both in separateness and in unity*

*Life can now be lived to its fullest
since each has extended capacity for love –
for relatedness – for further transformation*

*Each now knowing how to harness
the energy of love can now enhance
the being of the Other*

*This is done by accepting the uniqueness of the Other –
both strengths and weaknesses of the Other –
thereby accepting unconditionally
the divineness of the Other*

*If we are able to do this
indeed we are able to experience Agape – Love*

Nothing could be sweeter

∞

Emerging from an Act of Betrayal

*In an intimate relationship we certainly will encounter
different facets of ourselves than we do with folk
with whom we are not so deeply involved*

*Some of these facets of who we are
may bring us and our partner joy
but others can bring us nasty consequences
that we would rather avoid*

*One such situation is when we have done some act
that has deeply wounded our partner
but we fail to appreciate the magnitude of distress
that we have caused our loved one*

*One such act is betrayal
In some manner we have done an act that has altered
the basic trust that existed prior to the act of betrayal
and yet we fail to understand the degree of suffering
that we have caused our partner*

*At that time we may say "I am sorry"
and then expect our relationship to go on
as if nothing ever happened*

*But if we do expect that to happen
we may be in for a rude awakening
Letting go of a state of being wounded
is not on a set time table*

*Each of us has our own personal history of prior wounds
This history is crucial in how we find recovery
from our state of woundedness*

*If this process of recovery takes longer
than the offender thinks it should
then he/she may begin to say to the wounded one
" I told you that I was sorry – now get over it"*

*Needless to say this is not an effective strategy
and may just prolong the "letting go" process
because the wounded one's basic need to
be heard and responded to with kindness and
compassion is not taking place*

*When we have been wounded we need for
someone to hear our cry of distress
and to take some action to aid us in the process of
getting relief from our suffering*

*Part of this process is for the offender to take
responsibility for having wounded his/her partner*

*An additional step that is needed to reestablish trust
is to reassure the partner that effort will be
made to assist in the healing process*

*That assistance often involves the offender
taking steps to change his/her behavior
in order to avoid a reoccurrence of
further wounding the partner*

*Now this is a tall order because it calls for the offender to
function from a higher state of being than Ego
It calls for the offender to function at the higher states of
being as Observer-Witness Self or as Divine Self*

*Both of these components of Self enable us to put the
welfare of the partner before our own needs
but Ego is unable to do this*

*Ego is so concerned about its own perceived threats
that it cannot place the needs of the partner first*

*When we function as Observer-Witness Self
we gain a more objective understanding of
what we are doing in a relationship and
avoid blaming the partner*

*On the other hand when we function as Ego –
operating from a lower state – we often will continue to
deny taking responsibility for causing harm
to the partner and will also blame the partner
for all that is going wrong in the relationship*

*When we function as Divine Self – rather than Ego –
we are able to feel compassion for the partner and
to desire to do what we can to alleviate the suffering that
we – as the offender – have brought about*

*This compassion and this desire to take away the
suffering that we have caused – if both are truly genuine
and not just manipulative talk –
will have remarkable healing effects in the relationship*

*But how about the wounded one
Where is he/she in all of this process of betrayal*

*Well one of the main things that is needed is for the
offended one to realize what takes place within us
when we feel betrayed by our partner*

*First know that when we sense betrayal
this is interpreted immediately by our brain and body
as though we are in danger*

*Chemical/physiological changes are set in motion
to prepare for us to do battle and fight
or else to flee from the threat*

*Part of this reaction is often an obsessive rumination
playing and replaying disturbing thoughts
concerning the act of the perceived betrayal*

*Not infrequently these painful ruminations
involve feelings of anger/hatred toward the offender
as well as a loss of feelings of self-worth
and value for oneself*

*Unless resolved quickly depression follows with a
sense of confusion and an inability to think clearly
or to act decisively to protect one's sense of self-worth*

*Again what is needed here is for the offended one
to be able to function from a position of
safety and strength rather than from fear and weakness*

*In order to do this the offended one
must move from functioning primarily as Ego
and assume the higher states
of Observer-Witness Self and Divine Self*

*If he/she can make this transition then it is much easier
to let go of this terrible state of suffering
and to regain the feelings of self-value –
self-worth – and self-love*

*Once these are back then he/she can more easily decide
what to do about the relationship and how to let go of the
hatred/bitterness that came with the betrayal*

*The process of forgiveness is an
important element in this difficult process
It cannot come about if one is functioning as Ego
It can come about if one is functioning as Divine Self*

*Being able to function as Divine Self involves being
receptive to God's grace and love that is being offered
as well as a desire on our part to assume this role even
though we may not be exactly sure we know how to do it*

*Certainly patience and persistence on our part
will be required but perhaps the most important element
will be to learn the act of self-compassion*

∞

'Tis a Gift

'Tis a gift to be honest
'Tis a gift to be true
'Tis a gift to be the authentic you

You've listened to the message
of your heart and soul

You've reclaimed all parts of Self
and once again have become whole

As you continue on your sacred quest
just remember
all of life is blessed

So shine shine shine
ever good and true

It's no wonder that
we love you like we do

∞

Chapter 2: Finding Secrets Within

A Secret No More

*What if all the great mystics of the world
shared a common secret*

A secret about how to experience the Divine

*What if Jesus and Buddha shared this same secret
What if this secret could be known by you and by me*

The secret can now be told

*To experience the Divine we simply enter a
Meditative State*

*Some may call it an altered way of being
Jesus called it the Kingdom of God
The Kingdom of God in the Now
So simple – yet so powerful
So close – so attainable
For you – for me*

*In this Present moment
It is within you – it is within me
Yours to have – mine to have*

*Achievable in various ways
Meditation – Prayer – Imagination – Chanting
The technique is not important*

In this Meditative State we become receptive
We open ourselves to a new way of being

In this Meditative State
we experience a Spiritual Reality
The Reality of Soul – the Reality of Spirit
Really just the Reality of the pure Now

In this State our perception changes

Our memory changes – our beliefs change –
even our identity changes

In this State we experience God/dess
So powerful – yet so peaceful
So redemptive – so transformative
So temporary – so enduring

In this State Ego submits to Self
In this State Self submits to God/dess
In this State my light merges with the Light
In this State there is Oneness – Wholeness

∞

George W. Barnard M.D.

Seeking an Anchor

*All of us need some kind of anchor
so that in a time of storm and crisis
we do not feel alone*

*For some this anchor can be a person –
a spiritual figure – a Meditative State
Whatever we choose we want this force near us*

*This means that we need to know
how to contact and engage this meaningful energy*

I will share what works best for me

*First I close my eyes in order to turn inward
I need to be more attentive to what is occurring in my
mind rather than what is occurring in the
external world around me*

*In order to make this transition I silently focus on
my breathing – making sure that my exhalations are for a
longer period of time than are my inhalations*

*This move assures that my Modern Myelinated Vagus is
getting me into a Parasympathetic mode
rather than a Sympathetic one
This helps to relax my body
If needed I will do a body scan to further
enhance body relaxation*

*Next I begin to use both imagination and visualization
I begin an internal dialogue with my brain*

I may start with a simple visualization
For instance I may say to my imagination
"Carry me back to a time when I was very relaxed
Let me see myself as I was then and see others as
they were then but at the same time as
Observer-Witness Self let me look on as I am now"
This maneuver permits me to function
both as participant and as observer

Still speaking to my imagination
"Now going back in time where I was extremely relaxed
permit my whole body and mind to recall
in detail how it felt

Let each cell tap its memory and recall how it was
functioning at that time and then permit that
state of functioning to exist in the present moment"

Speaking again to my imagination

"If you will – permit me to return to a time when I was
able to leave my plane mode of being wherein I was
functioning primarily as Ego and move to a higher mode
of being wherein I can function primarily as Divine Self"

Functioning in this mode I am able to let go of being
almost exclusively preoccupied about satisfying
my own needs and instead I am able to be more concerned
about fulfilling the needs of the Other

"Now take me back in time to an occasion when I was
unable clearly to understand and appreciate
the needs of the Other

George W. Barnard M.D.

*But this time as I relive this occasion
let it be different
This time let me have empathy
This time let me feel compassion*

*Let my actions reflect that the needs of the Other are
being heard and acted on with understanding
Let my facial expressions reflect love and concern
Let my voice show tenderness and caring*

*As I function in this mode in the presence of the Other
let my body and my mind become aware of this
mode of being so that in the future I may return to this
mode of being more freely and permit me to stay in this
mode of functioning for a longer period of time"*

*Realizing that I can reach this goal more easily
with the assistance of a higher power than I am
I request that the Divine Spirit be with me
and lend me wisdom – understanding – patience*

*Silently I remain in this frame of mind for a short
period of time and then gently
I assume my usual mode of being
still carrying with me the brain and body memories
and integration of functioning from a
higher mode of being than normal*

∞

Expanding My Boundaries

Let me access a Meditative State

*Experience reality as it is from the
viewpoint of the dreamer – the artist
With vivid certainty see the universe as being right
just as it is – at this moment*

*Lose my sense of boundaries
In my imagination let my being expand
Let it unfold to become the whole
All is one*

*Let me experience it as
this is the way it has always been – and will be
The cosmos and I are one*

*Let me be aware of being more than body
Experience the pure pleasure of being –
in this moment – Now
Experience the fullness – the completeness –
the wholeness in being – Now*

*As energy feel myself as light so
I can penetrate darkness and gain primordial wisdom
Feel myself as water so I can seep into the cracks of
my Soul and experience its depth and beauty*

*Experience the union of Divine Self with Divine Spirit
The joy of oneness is mine*

∞

George W. Barnard M.D.

Birthing the Stone

*She approached the stone with caution –
with awe – with reverence*

*What mysteries lay within its core
What secrets lay disguised
before this wondering stone sculptor
How could she ever decipher
the hidden unknown*

*Then it came to her
This raw stone was no different than her Soul*

*It too had its secrets – its mysteries
It too offered a challenge
to be understood – to be appreciated – to be revealed*

*Whether she approaches the mysteries
of the stone – or her Soul
she must turn inward
she must learn to listen to her intuitive voice*

*The voice that utters no sound
yet speaks such a clear message of wisdom
revealing the secrets – the beauty –
the potential that lie deeply embedded within*

*As she proceeded to chip away
how she envied the honey bee that seemed to
know so well how to perform its miraculous task*

Unlocking Life's Secrets

Yet she had no such defined instincts
to guide her with certainty

She could only use her imagination –
her dreams – her hunches
to guide her on this journey as she fearlessly
stripped away the non-meaningful
in order to expose the true essence that was within

Her task was to surrender herself
to the inner truth of the stone
and to let it unfold
as she lovingly chipped away at the stone –
or was it her Soul

She certainly encountered doubts
and she definitely met resistances
But she continued to listen – to have patience –
even compassion and forgiveness

Then one morning she blinked in amazement

The light of the sun
gently diffused itself through the stone
to reveal the beauty of the Goddess
that she had unearthed – had birthed

Was it stone - or was it Soul

Was there really a difference

∞

George W. Barnard M.D.

Encouraging Him On

*She had been with him in his dreams
Her presence had meant so much
But where was she today*

*Today was an important time in his life
Today was the 26 mile marathon
He had never done anything like this before
Was he up to it – today*

*It was 3 a.m. – the air was cold
but his body was warm with excitement*

*As he began the course his eyes were drawn
to the woman in the purple body suit just ahead of him
Watching her movements should
keep him preoccupied for awhile*

*Then her pace slowed
She dropped back – next to him –
Their strides synchronized
She asked if she could run with him
"Sure" – he said - and on they ran
No other words spoken but their breathing was as one*

*Mile after mile and before he knew it
they were at mile sixteen
"That's all I can do" – she said
as she dropped out of the race*

Unlocking Life's Secrets

*Although she was gone
her presence remained with him
as he journeyed on*

Who was she – why did she show up today

*Then he remembered
He had met her before in his dreams
She had the same blonde hair –
the same blue eyes – the same teasing smile*

*The Goddess of the night – his Goddess
She had been there encouraging him on
by setting the pace*

*In fact she was there still – encouraging him on
as he crossed the finish line*

∞

George W. Barnard M.D.

Experiencing Being

*When I go into the unknown of my unconscious
and function as Observer-Witness Self –
with detachment –
I meet demons previously unfamiliar to me
or meet once again those tormentors of my Soul
I have known so well before*

*I identify them – but do not identify with them
I accept them as being a part of me but they are not me*

*In this way I open myself to a new way of being –
to a new way of experiencing*

*I can experience fear without being terrified/paralyzed
I can experience sorrow without being overwhelmed
I can experience suffering without being devastated*

*I can experience shame without
identifying myself as being bad*

*I can experience being without boundaries –
without limitations*

I experience being as part of Being

∞

Finding a Safe Haven

*All of us need a safe place
A place where we can become quiet and restored
Therefore let me use my imagination*

*Let me visualize myself in a clear bubble
that can float about at my will*

*Inside this magic bubble I am invisible to others
Here if I choose I can simply be
I don't have to do
Here I can relax and be replenished
by the Universe's loving Life Forces*

*This is a sacred place for me
because it is here that my fragmented being
becomes unified – integrated by mysterious means
that I don't fully understand
but that I still appreciate greatly*

*Often I take the time to enter
a Meditative State
in order to relax my body and mind
I close my eyes – take in several deep breaths*

*And then I do a body scan
in which I systematically focus my attention
on different parts of my body –
beginning with the muscles in my right foot*

*I take a deep breath in and then I slowly exhale –
making sure that my period of exhalation is
3-4 times longer than my inhalation
This maneuver will stimulate my Parasympathetic
Nervous System and help me relax*

*I allow the muscles in my right foot
to become loose and free of tension
I repeat the process with my left foot*

*Slowly and gradually
I move my attention up my body –
focusing my attention on relaxing the muscles
of my legs – thighs – pelvis – lower back – upper back –
across my chest – my shoulders – arms – hands –
around my eyes – my neck – face and scalp*

*Now with my body relaxed
my mind also becomes quiet and still*

*In this Meditative State
I can remain in my balloon
and as Observer-Witness Self
simply watch my thoughts in detachment
or I can revisit my past – step out of my balloon
and re-experience past events
but from a different perspective*

*In this Meditative State I can think and feel as I did then
but at the same time – in detachment
I can split off as Observer-Witness Self wherein
I do not carry the painful conditioning from the past but
approach problem solving from a
more rational perspective*

*This approach allows me to break old cycles of behavior
that carry destructive elements with them*

*Thus in my imagination –
but which my brain sees as reality –
I can engage in a process wherein new neuronal tracts are
laid down that are more adaptive than
the previous ones I had*

*When I am ready to leave this Meditative State
I open my eyes and take a minute or so to move my
attention back to my ordinary state of being –
carrying with me the belief that I have
gained more self-regulatory control and integration*

∞

George W. Barnard M.D.

Having Self-Compassion

*Why is it so hard for some of us to have compassion
- Karuna - for ourselves*

*Sometimes it seems that it is easier for us
to have compassion for a friend – or even a stranger –
than it is to have compassion for ourselves*

*When we have compassion we have mercy
or we show kindness to the suffering*

*Why is it so hard to show compassion to ourselves
Maybe – just maybe –
we can't acknowledge that we are in pain –
or maybe we believe that we are in pain but think that
we are undeserving of kindness – of forgiveness*

*If I wish to I can re-experience
someone deeply caring for me and
showing their compassion for me –
whether I felt deserving or not*

*I first enter a Meditative State
After I am in this Meditative State
I ask my imaginative mind to take me back in time
to an occasion when I was suffering and
someone who knew this and cared for me deeply
wished for me to have relief and
experience happiness and well-being*

*Let me visualize this compassionate person
accepting me as I was*

*When I am in the presence of this loving being
I permit myself to feel attuned to him/her
Their presence is emitting loving kindness to me*

*I feel my burdens lifted
as I relax and soak in this gift freely bestowed on me
I feel how easy it is to breathe*

*It is as though the chains around
my chest have been removed*

*Compassion has a gentle way of caressing us
in order to quieten our inner turmoil*

*In this moment I experience this calming effect
I delight in this restorative effect
Once again I feel free
Once again I feel whole*

*In the future I may not always feel this way
But certainly now that I have experienced it
I know how to return to this refreshing spring
any time that my Soul is feeling dry
and is in need of wetness*

*Having received compassion from another
in the future I can use this as
a model for showing compassion to myself*

George W. Barnard M.D.

*This is my personal oasis and I may return here
as often as I need to do so*

This is my path to self-compassion

*After basking here for a bit
I return to my usual mode of being
carrying with me a great sense of being worthy –
a great sense of feeling accepted by another –
of being cared for by another –
of knowing how to receive compassion from another
and how to give compassion to myself and to the Other*

∞

Inward Bound

*The external world could no longer nourish me
so that my Soul did not hunger*

*With meditation I went inward
to feed my spiritual barrenness*

*This Meditative State gave me the healing water
my parched Soul desired*

*It was in this Meditative State
that myth – ritual – intuition – imagination
sowed seeds in a fertile soil*

*My journey towards wholeness
was a journey of transformation –
my transformation*

*Really a journey to find
balance and integration of the inner forces –
not only with themselves –
but also with the external world*

*To walk this path I learned to focus
less on the external world
and learn to experience my inner reality*

*What I sought was knowledge of the Self –
my gnosis – my knowing
It was here I found my fullness of being –
which led to authentic living*

George W. Barnard M.D.

*My metanoia – my turning around –
began when I put emphasis both
on the knowledge I obtain from the senses
as well as that which I obtain from the heart*

*Before I experienced this fullness though
I first had to taste my own alienation and walk through
the cave of darkness and terror*

*It was here I met my Shadow Self –
my Destructive Self – carrying its baskets of
cruelty – meanness – greed – envy*

*As I sampled these I had to
walk through the valley of fear – dread – sorrow*

*This was not an easy journey so I expected my Soul
to feel bruised and sore from my struggles*

*At times I thought I had made progress
but the slope was slippery and frequently
I found myself lying in the mud of despair*

*To take this journey demanded I take the risk of feeling
as though I had fallen into an endless pit of loneliness*

*Then I remembered spiritual growth is a continuing
process that demands my daily involvement
lest the weeds of rationality and materialism crowd out
my fragile plant of the non-rational
as it struggled for survival*

*I needed not think that this mysterious
sacred journey of mine consisted only of suffering
or that my path was filled only with
stones and briars that tear at my Soul*

*What it did mean was that this journey for meaning
is rooted in my inner experiences
and in my cavern of the unconscious
There are powerful forces with which I had to wrestle*

*I was determined not to be intimidated because
I had inner allies of strength
who would make the journey with me
Among these were Wisdom Self – Observer-Witness Self
Defender/Protector Self and Divine Self*

*These components of the Self were
my constant companions and guides
on my journey toward wholeness
as I confronted my Shadow-Destructive Self*

*They led me when I seemed lost –
protected me when I was threatened –
comforted me when I was fearful or felt overwhelmed –
and gave me loving compassion when I felt
ashamed – unworthy – alienated – homesick*

*These allies have authentic creativity and power which
become my authentic creativity and
my authentic power as I seek to integrate
my conscious and unconscious forces
in my search for meaning*

George W. Barnard M.D.

*As the hidden mysterious energies within become active
they will have an imprint on me that is apparent and felt*

*I will be curious about who I am in all my complexity and
be receptive to who I may become as I mine
the rich ores of transformation –
redemption – healing – unification*

∞

Experiencing the Numinous

How do I unravel the mysteries of God
Do I soar to the heavens – or descend to the seas
How far out do I have to explore to reach the Divine

I must quit my search outward
Call a halt to this journey for it will be in vain

Instead I go to the silence within

I leave my senses – abandon my intellect –
discard my reasoning
These are only needless armors
that will weigh me down
I must go beyond this excess baggage

On my inward journey I travel lightly – nakedly
wearing only my garment of experience

I become accustomed to the darkness within
since the Beloved loves to dance in the shadows

I learn to listen to the deep silence
because the Master's message may not come in words
I prepare myself to live with paradox
because the Teacher transcends duality

I expect to come away feeling joyful and fulfilled
because the Divine Spirit consists of love
and shares Essence with essence

∞

George W. Barnard M.D.

Journey of Change

*I look for the challenge of being – of becoming
I shake security from my Soul
as I emerge from my safe cocoon*

*For years I have been told by others about God
My world has been certain
I have known what to expect*

*But now is the time for spiritual growth –
my spiritual growth
I must take that scary – but vital – step*

*I want to experience God/dess for myself –
not following someone else's path
but taking my own unique journey*

*Since childhood others have painted
the picture of the Divine One
I now desire my own experience – my own dharma*

*As a snake sheds its old skin to reveal the new
now I shed my old beliefs to reveal
those discovered by me*

*Both cautiously and boldly I take the first step
not sure of what I will find*

*Will God/dess hear my call
Will the Divine One reveal the Godself to me
Will God/dess welcome my desire for contact
Or is rejection waiting*

Unlocking Life's Secrets

What if I can't fly
What if I fall to the ground
These and other thoughts go through my mind

Then I remember
Every eagle that has flown has faced these questions
as it tumbles from the nest
only then to spread its wings –
to soar through the clouds
The eagle has to trust

I have to trust –
trust my inner being – my inner wisdom
trust the inner Being – the inner Wisdom
to be my faithful guides
on my journey of change

Change is my constant companion
Change knew me before I had a body
Change will know me when I return to soil
Change is both my being and my becoming

I am never alone

∞

George W. Barnard M.D.

Kundalini

Let me tap my underground stream

Let me kindle my internal flame

Let me be the spark point of my Soul

Let me be the cream for my strawberries

Let my early morning rooster crow

∞

Path to Freedom

*I felt alienated from my true being
My spiritual vision seemed dim – veiled
My awareness of Self was cloudy
My heart felt barren – cold
I lacked wisdom – understanding*

So what was I to do

*First I directed my attention – my efforts – inward
as I entered a Meditative State
to discover the secrets of life –
to plummet the mysteries of the Soul*

*It was here I was to explore my beliefs – my attitudes –
and ferret out the ones which were no longer true*

*They served a purpose for me earlier in life
but now needed to be transformed
I searched my inner being
to find that to which I grasped
to see how I was driven by my projections –
my unconscious compulsions*

*I faced my multitude of emotions –
including those of pain as well as those of joy*

*I came to grips with
my destructive – negative functions
as well as my constructive – creative ones*

George W. Barnard M.D.

*I sought repeatedly to reconcile – integrate
those moral opposites that have pulled me apart
In so doing I experienced my fullness of being –
my wholeness – my pleroma*

*It was in facing these inner forces
of darkness and light
that I was able to give up my homesickness –
my alienation*

∞

Chapter 3: Suffering and Healing

Approaching Retirement

Soon I would have to make a decision
Should I – or should I not –
enter the phased retirement program

For thirty years this job had been my life –
at least a major part of it

During my work career
I had been through a series of struggles

I had fought some of my battles well
I could feel good about my accomplishments
But the successes in my career had come at a price

I had found it necessary to deny attention – time – effort
to my own personal development –
my own spiritual growth –
my own identity

Who was I really

Who was this person
behind the professional mask

Outside my job
what meaning did life offer me

Without the dictates of my job
how would I structure my time

George W. Barnard M.D.

*Could my wife and I really be together –
in peace – for long periods each day*

Only time would tell

Postscript

*I am happy to say that we have done well
during the retirement years*

*My wife and I took off in our motor home
and were gone for four months*

*This gave us time to adjust to a different time plan
and for me to be involved in activities other than work*

∞

Walking from the Cave of Darkness

*Am I a closet anorexic starving myself of
spiritual nourishment –
becoming drained of my zest for life*

*Have I been snared into the deadly web of judgment –
struggling like the helpless fly caught in the web –
to set myself free*

In either case I am but the victim of deceit

*I have been deceived
by my strivings for perfection
which loudly proclaim my basic unworthiness –
just as I am*

*It parcels out morsels of conditional love
only if I meet its strict demands*

*Let me open my heart
Let it overflow with love and compassion –
to ignite once again my own internal divine light*

*Allow it to shine without a flicker
as I walk from my cave of darkness*

*Let the cold shadows of self-rejection
melt before the warm glow of acceptance*

I rejoice in my worthiness

∞

George W. Barnard M.D.

Connection to the Primal

*Let my heart open
like a flower unfolding its petals
to the early morning sun*

*Let my mind become still
like the silence of a deep cave*

*Let my Soul become trusting
like a child cradled
in the arms of its mother*

*Let my Spirit carry me
like an eagle with its wings spread
gliding gracefully through the canyon*

*Let my tongue speak the truth
like an arrow shot from a bow*

*Let my inner voice guide me to healing
like the church bell sounding its sacred tone*

∞

Unlocking Life's Secrets

Sharing Life's Breath

*If I let go of my sense of self-importance
I let go of a heavy burden*

*My load becomes light
I am guilt-free
I float into death
I jump into life
I experience my essence daily*

*If I then communicate with the Other
the truth of who I am
I honor my own value – my worth*

*I then can share my life's breath
only to experience my inner being transform
to become the breath of life*

*I open my doors so the sunlight within
mingles with the rain without
and a rainbow is born to be enjoyed with the Other*

∞

George W. Barnard M.D.

Inner Transformation

*For some years I have struggled with
the issue of my inner transformation*

*If I am to grow I must let old parts of me die
Old concepts that are false
Old concepts that are destructive
Old concepts that limit my potential*

*I ask myself
How do I let go of the old me - my limited Ego
to find my new – limitless Self*

*The Ego includes only the conscious part of me
whereas the Self includes both
the conscious and unconscious parts of me
It is from the unconscious that I will tap my essence
It is from here that I will discover my true being*

*I need to:
Lower the barrier that
separates me from this eternal source
Balance the forces of the conscious and unconscious
Subordinate the Ego to the Self
Become receptive to the divine forces within me
Tap my sacred power which for
too long has been dormant
Let the Self's task of unifying
opposites become my goal
Balance the polarities
Experience the divine*

∞

Mythic Journey

When did it happen
When did my sense of Soul shut down
When did I lose contact with the Divine Child within

Oh beloved little one who wounded your Soul –
when it was so fresh and so eager to be
Who shamed you into conformity
and put your enthusiasm asleep

How did it happen – that you became nonconscious –
unaware of who you are – deep inside

Who shut down your imagination – your creativity
Who was the tyrant that gave you tongue lashings –
so as to dampen your warrior spirit –
by killing your inner dragon
Who stole your royal heritage from you

Come with me now on my mythic journey
so that I may find that long lost Divine Child
Someone may have stolen
my Pole Star – the ordered – stable one

I may have to journey
to the underworld of darkness to find it

This is a treacherous land
Many demons guard the gates to the Golden Kingdom
so I call on my experienced inner guides
to show me the way

George W. Barnard M.D.

*As I descend the steps into darkness
I feel afraid – I feel helpless to yet unknown forces*

*But I do not identify with fear –
with helplessness – with sorrow – with rage*

I am more

*These are but feelings from my childhood years
Let my brain remember my suffering
but this time my body does not recoil
to the pain as before –
because as Observer-Witness Self I become detached
and in my imagination watch from the safe position
inside my protective bubble*

*From this secure place I am able to relive
the trauma – the suffering of those times
when my life's functions
were determined by Another*

*When my will was not my will –
but the will of the Other*

*As I relive these moments I realize
that in my suffering – my woundedness
my Soul was not killed
My inner Divine Child has only been asleep
It lives – to be reclaimed – by me*

*So I look around in the darkness –
for the light – for the fire*

*From its flames I see the Firebird arise
and bid me to climb aboard*

*Soaring from the darkness – carrying me into the light
I realize I am not the same*

*This initiation into the world of darkness
has transformed me – rebirthed me –
really reunited me to my natural heritage –
my sense of worthiness – of belonging
The Firebird delivers me home*

*Awaiting me is my Divine Self who says
"Welcome home beloved child
Welcome Divine Child"
Into the outstretched arms of gentleness
I allow myself – Body and Soul –
to be nestled in the bosom of this Loving One*

*I feel recognized – accepted – honored – cherished –
perhaps accepted for the first time –
for my own divine uniqueness –
without any Masks – without any armoring defenses –
even with my Shadow Self present –
with all its nastiness – with all its negativity –
yes – even with all its destructiveness*

*Hallelujah – what relief – what comfort
Having awakened from my deadened state –
my twilight sleep –
I am now connected with Life Force –
with Firebird Energy – with Ka*

George W. Barnard M.D.

*Once again my cells remember how to feel
I now have my freedom
I let go of my restrictions – my constrictions*

*I will use my renewed energy to break the deadly hold
that Judgmental Self has had on my voice
As I wish – I will cry out in pain - sob in sorrow
or shout my ecstasy – my joy
I loudly proclaim my worthiness
I let my Soul extol its lovableness*

*Then quietly – gently – I let every cell in my body
drop the fear – the terror – adopted so long ago
I deny Judgmental Self the right to keep me paralyzed*

*In this wonderful moment – this present Now –
I experience this exuberant delight –
this almost overwhelming joy*

*Even the cells within that almost withered away –
now flourish in recognition of my new-found authenticity
– my genuine Self – my center*

*These cells recognize they have not been abandoned –
as previously feared
Now they bubble with life-renewed energy
of non-judgmental acceptance – even being imperfect*

*The cells dance all night in celebration
of what the future holds*

I rejoice – I rejoice in Wholeness

∞

Prisoner in My Own Being

Perhaps you are like me – then again perhaps not

*There are times from my childhood
when I vividly recall a painful scene
but I can't get any feelings to go with it*

*Yet I so know the destructive elements must be there
because I see indirect evidence with footprints of
Sorrow – Rage – Abandonment – Helplessness*

*These painful emotions or their effects
are displaced toward the wrong people
or they are shown in inappropriate ways
Why this disassociation
Because the pain came too early
The pain was too strong for my Child Self to handle*

*Where were my parents when I needed them
Where was the protection
Where was the comfort – the reassurance
I feel so cheated
The cells of my body remember the pain –
but not my conscious awareness*

*How do I get out of this prison
How do I obtain my freedom*

*The first step is for my Adult Self
to become a parent for my Child Self
Then and only then will my Child Self feel safe*

*Now I let the anti-stress hormone Oxytocin
flow freely from Adult Self
surrounding Child Self with love/acceptance
reassuring Child Self that she/he is safe*

*If done over a period of time
healing will take place*

Postscript – Years later

Good News!!

The integration process did work

*I was able to feel safe enough
to experience a lot of painful emotions
and also some very joyful ones*

I am no longer a prisoner

*As a free man I can now deeply feel
both negative and positive emotions
and I can claim ownership of them*

They are part of me but I am more

Indeed the journey toward wholeness is worthwhile

∞

Lifting the Veil from Childhood Emotions

*Sometimes I experience the world
as friendly – trustworthy – reliable
Sometimes as hostile – cruel – undependable*

*It makes a difference in whether
I feel safe – secure – capable – courageous
or helpless – fearful – estranged – vulnerable*

*To solve this riddle I need to remember my childhood –
that critical time of my life
when I was first learning to be me –
when I was learning the difference
between me and the other
when my wishes were not in keeping
with mother – with father*

How did they tell me no

*What was the look on the face
What was the tone of voice as they set limits on me –
on what I could do – or could not do*

*Did they yell in anger – with a scowling face
or soothe and reassure with a friendly smile
as they denied my wishes – or failed to meet my demands*

*Did they maintain my faith or lose my trust in their love
as they judged my behavior and determined
what was right and what was wrong*

They had the power – they had the control –
in this struggle over me –
in this conflict over my thoughts –
my shoulds and my should nots

How did they express this power – this superiority

Their control over me – especially in early years –
was formative – even life determining

It was they who determined
what I was fed – and when I received it
when I was held and when I was comforted
when my cries – even my calls of distress – were heard
and how they were responded to

It is from the root of these life experiences
that we form our basic beliefs –
toward ourselves – toward others –
toward God – toward life

It is from these early interactions with our parents
that we form our attitudes of:
trust versus distrust
hope versus hopelessness
courage versus fear
love versus hate

As infants – as children – we were helpless
We depended on our parents
for nurturance – for protection – for guidance

*Even before we learned to speak
we received messages from the tone of voice –
from the facial expression of our parents –
from the way they touched us*

*When we were frightened – how did they reassure
When we were lonely or sad – how did they comfort
When we were needy –
how did they attend to – or ignore us
When we upset/frustrated our parents –
how did they show anger*

*Somewhere deep within each of us are
these implicit – unconscious memories
They may not be accessible to our awareness
but they are there and play an active role*

*Our memories may be true only in part
but they have been powerful –
influential in the development of our belief system*

*It is from this belief system that we develop
our attitudes toward self – toward others*

*Some of our attitudes may be right and some wrong
It is from our wrong attitudes that we develop
much of our suffering in life*

*I need to remember this because many of my beliefs –
my attitudes – were formed
before my brain was fully developed*

George W. Barnard M.D.

*This means I may have operated on mistaken ideas
or unsound emotions –
which led me to conflict and distress*

*On my journey of self-discovery
it is my task to ferret out these false beliefs –
to see how my mistaken attitudes have caused me
to inaccurately judge my strengths and my weaknesses*

*How do I approach this difficult task
First I need to allow some of my unconscious barriers
to be lifted so I may become aware
of my hidden conflicts and painful memories*

*I do this by analyzing my dreams
or accessing a Meditative State
through meditation – imagination –
contemplative prayer*

*Once this state of being is reached
I recall a memory from my adulthood
that was especially painful – for example a time wherein
I was very fearful of another person*

*I then visualize that scene – I recall how my body felt
At the same time – as my Observer-Witness Self –
I watch this process in a detached manner
Then I allow that scene to disappear*

*While still holding on to the state of fear
I allow my imaginative mind to return me
to a time in my childhood when I felt this same terror –
perhaps a time with my father – or my mother*

*I allow the child within once again to recall
the facial expressions – to see the eyes –
experienced as judging and condemning
or to listen to the voice –
heard as harsh and threatening*

*But this time the fear does not paralyze the child
because Defender-Protector Self stands beside the child
giving it courage – giving it security –
giving it reassurance*

*With this support I now have the strength
to experience a basic source of my fears*

This has a healing effect on my body – on my soul

*It gives me the courage to use this approach
in order to explore other emotions –
negative ones of anger – hatred – sorrow – loneliness
as well as positive ones of joy – love – compassion*

*It is in this way that I lift the veils before my eyes
so I may experience the world as it was – as it is*

*Even of greater importance to me
I come to understand myself and how I came to be*

This gives me freedom now to become a different me

∞

George W. Barnard M.D.

Moving On

*As he came to lock his office door
he paused and looked around – so many memories -
twenty-five years of memories
now coming to an end*

*His research software company – where so many nights –
so many weekends – claimed him as their own
now coming to an end*

The choice was not his

*His company had been bought by a large firm
They had promised to keep his company going
but cash flow problems emerged
They had opportunity to sell for cash and sell they did*

*But how about the engineers –
the programmers – the secretary
All gone – no longer needed
The software was all that counted – it brought the cash
His heart was heavy as he locked the door
for the last time*

*What was he to do – what was in store for him
He knew what was needed but was he up to it*

*Could he face the suffering – the needed suffering
It was his pain – his grief*

*It was his company that died
And now he must let it go*

*He must mourn its death
as though a part of him had died
In fact – a part of him had died
But that was what gave him hope*

*As he looked inward – as he explored his emptiness
he also found his anger – his resentment – his bitterness
all lurking in his dark alleys – trying to entrap him*

But he trudged on

*He had been in this cave before
Demons residing here were no stranger to him
so he journeyed on
Even shaving his beard as he went*

*If he was to be transformed on this journey of death
he wanted some choices*

*He knew he had to shed old images – old memories –
as he grieved and moved on –*

*If he was to live in the NOW
he must give up his old being*

If his new Self was to live his old Ego must let go

This was the true meaning of his healing process

∞

George W. Barnard M.D.

Entering My Sacred Space

*How long have I been exiled
from my homeland – my Center*

*How long have I been
stranded in the desert – that barren land
where there is no spark to my Soul*

*I have searched for the oasis –
for the land of flowing waters*

*Come – let me enter my sacred space –
unbound by time*

*Come – let me enter the sacred temple within –
that holy space that existed from time eternal
It is here the sacred mysteries reside
Here there is no set doctrinal creed*

*Here I seek my own understanding – my gnosis –
my knowing from my own experiences
This is my well of wisdom – of truth*

*In my silence I listen for the inner voices
that share the Divine Unknown
It is here I walk through the wilderness –
in the land of Shadows*

*I eat and sleep with my darkness
Without yielding – there is acceptance*

*It is here I enter
the furnace of transformation
to burn away the impurities
which mask my inner golden Self*

*As I get in touch with the unconscious –
as I bring Self in harmony
with the unseen order of Universal Self
then I notice a change in me*

*Tenseness – worry – are gone
replaced by equanimity and inner peace*

*As I lose identification with Ego
and gain identification with Self
there is a spiritual renewal – a transformation in me*

*My new vision permits me to experience a connection yes
even an ongoing relationship –
of Self with Universal Self*

*This partnership – this co-creatorship
determines the course of life's destiny –
creative evolution of the present moment*

*Freedom to choose –
Freedom to be –
my Ultimate Self*

*To achieve my innate potential
as being is melded with Being*

George W. Barnard M.D.

This is where life's ultimate meaning is to be found

*Opposites are united
My uniqueness and my sameness
are experienced in the same moment*

*Fragmentation dissolves into Wholeness
Meaninglessness becomes Meaning
Separateness disappears into Unity*

∞

Forgiveness Is Mine

For many of us self-forgiveness is extremely difficult

*Why are we so hard on ourselves
Why must we insist on holding onto our suffering*

*Our suffering with guilt and shame certainly does
nothing to repair the damage we have caused the Other*

*Short-term guilt – feeling bad about our actions –
can cause us to be more reflective so that in the future
we may be more vigilant regarding our behavior*

*Shame is feeling bad about ourselves –
basically equating ourselves with our actions
We feel that if we performed bad actions
we are a bad person*

*Shame is never good because shame is destructive
Holding onto long-term guilt can be very destructive
because it chronically eats away at our Soul*

*Both guilt and shame destroy our inner being
as they attack our self-acceptance*

*So how do we let go of these vicious monsters
How do we learn to have compassion and
forgiveness for ourselves*

*First we realize that this is not a task
that Ego is capable of doing
This requires a higher state of our being
This is a job for Divine Self*

George W. Barnard M.D.

*Divine Self can empathize
but Ego cannot*

*Divine Self can feel with the suffering Other
and wants him/her to be free of suffering
Ego cannot*

*Divine Self has the power to heal
Ego does not*

*Divine Self acting as an agent for God
has the power to bestow grace upon us*

*We don't earn grace
It is given as an act of unconditional love*

*When we receive and accept this Divine love
we understand that we are accepted
just as we are by the Divine*

*There is no need for guilt and shame
We have been released from bondage*

*Now our love can flow
Now we can pass this healing love on to the Other
Now we can have compassion and forgiveness
both for ourselves and for the Other*

Oh what Joy

∞

Gaining Access to Healing Memories

While we may not remember –
our body does

In a way it is not just our brain that has a memory
our body and all of its components also remember

And these memories can be captured
and re-experienced by us

This is a very valuable asset to have as we attempt
to regulate our minds and our bodies

Since these body memories are implicit
and therefore not at a conscious state of awareness
we need to enter a Meditative State
in order to gain access to them

But once we have this access then we can begin to
use these memories for self-healing purposes

The basic procedure is simple and can be used
for a great number of situations

I sit comfortably in a chair with my eyes closed

I am willing to relax my mind – brain – body unit
Now I focus my attention on my breath
I breathe in through the nose
and breath out through the mouth

George W. Barnard M.D.

*With an attitude of relaxing
I begin to focus my attention on my right foot and leg
permitting the muscles to become calm and peaceful*

*Gradually I do a complete body scan
First moving up the right foot and leg and then the left*

*I progress up the body relaxing each group of muscles
from the toes to the top of my head*

*Next I pause and take in a few deep breaths
and with each breath I allow the mind to relax*

*I pause – breathe deeply – and ask my imaginative
mind to carry me back in time to a time
where I was having an experience or feeling
that I wish to experience again*

*Let's say for now it is to re-experience the time where
I was the most relaxed I have ever been in my life*

*I don't know how to do this
but my imaginative mind does*

*I see myself as I was then but at the same time
look on as the detached Observer-Witness Self*

*Now I permit my body and mind to feel as they did then
I look about and then I turn my attention away from the
external and turn inward so that
I can become aware of various sensations
or body feelings that I may be having*

*I especially note my muscles and
feel the deep sense of relaxation*

*This is my time to relive this deep sense of peace
that goes with relaxation*

*I breathe deeply and feel the relaxation
I become aware of the heaviness of my body –
really the awesome sense of comfort
This is mine to enjoy and to experience as often as I desire*

*This is a healing experience – a reparative time for me -
a time to recover my inner balance
so that I may deal with stress more effectively*

*I remain here for a brief time and enjoy
the endorphins as they flow freely through my body*

*Then gently I relax and return
to the present moment – carrying with me
the sense of peace I have just experienced*

∞

George W. Barnard M.D.

I Ask Your Forgiveness

*Dear friend –
I come before you
asking your forgiveness*

*I know I have been long in coming –
I fought hard to deny how I had offended you*

*I tried to escape taking responsibility for my actions –
for wounding your Soul
But no matter where I ran Genuine Guilt
was breathing heavy on my heart*

*First I had to acknowledge –
then accept and take ownership of my wronging you*

*Oh how that hurt because my intent was not to harm –
but harm I did and now I suffer –
as I caused suffering to you*

*My request for forgiveness is threefold:
I seek forgiveness from you –
from God – and from myself*

Please hear my plea

∞

Letting Go of Old Tapes

*There I was in the midst of an argument
when BAM
something changed dramatically*

It wasn't anything I could express in words

*It was all nonverbal
Feelings – sensations – emotions
increased breathing – heart pounding – muscles tense*

Then awareness – I had been there before many years ago

*I was speaking words of anger
My voice was louder and my pace was faster than usual
I felt the need not only to defend myself
but also to say critical things of the Other*

*And when I focused in on the face of the Other
I could see pain – distress –
and this was not what I wanted*

*I paused – I took in several deep breaths
and let them out slowly*

*I was calling on the
Modern Myelinated Vagus and the
Orbital Medial Prefrontal Cortex
as well as Observer-Witness Self and Divine Self
for help and it came rapidly*

George W. Barnard M.D.

*I quickly realized that I was not just
engaging in an argument
but rather I was being deeply affected by
old non-conscious implicit memories –
really body memories –
of a stressful time from my distant past*

*They were causing me to function/behave
in a dysregulated way
and I needed to let go of these old tapes
Bingo – I did*

*In the blink of an eye I quickly changed my behavior
and so did the Other*

*Once the body language softened
once the voice tones and pitch became more relaxed
then we were both in the present
and not locked into old tapes from long ago*

*There was more rationality to our conversation
We resolved our differences and moved on*

What a marvelous relief

Now I am a believer

*My mind can change the regulation of my brain
and ultimately change my behavior*

∞

Maitri

*As my many layers of defense crumble
to reveal more of the real me –
even my Shadow Self that contains parts of me
that I find hard to accept –
I gasp in shock and disbelief*

*I try my usual response of denial – of rejection
of those fragments that I do not want to own
but in the background I hear the words
"Maitri – Maitri"*

*"What does this mean" – I say
"Who is this voice – the source of these words"*

"It is I – your Friend" – is the response

"And who is this" – I say

"Divine Self" – is the reply

*With this reassurance I relax to a degree
but still I feel perplexed*

"What does Maitri mean" – I persist

"I accept you just as you are " – comes the answer

*"Wow" I shout with glee
"You mean All of me"*

George W. Barnard M.D.

"All of you – Just as you are" – comes the affirmation

*This gives me joy – hope
If the Beloved can accept All of me
perhaps I can too*

*The process of unification of fragmented self has begun
Something new is alive in me – something delightful
Something called self-acceptance –
something called Self love*

*Ah Maitri – the compassionate heart opener
Shower me with your presence each day*

∞

Miracles Still Happen

He thought miracles only happened in the ancient past
That is until today

Today made him a believer – a strong believer
Because today it happened to him

For years he had been deaf in his right ear
Then today as he was driving along
the mysterious happened

Suddenly and without warning there was SOUND
Why now? Why me? – he asked

Then the tears rolled down his cheeks
And he questioned it no more

Indeed Miracles do still happen
And he was grateful

Now he knew the meaning of Grace
Now he knew the meaning of Joy

Not only does he hear in his right ear
As a bonus sometimes he hears
the Divine singing to him

Can there ever be a more constant
reminder of God's Presence

∞

George W. Barnard M.D.

My Heart Grew Hands

*In the middle of the night
my heart grew hands*

*So that they might hold you
when you are frightened*

Comfort you when you are in pain

*Give your parched mouth
a precious sip of water*

Wipe your tears when you are sad

Cook you a meal when you are hungry

Touch your cheek when you need the closeness of a friend

*Ah the power of the hands with their ability to touch –
to activate the production of Oxytocin -
that powerful anti-stress hormone
that can calm – heal – bond*

Thanks to the love and the power of the Divine

∞

Conquering Fear

*Betty was a 48 year old successful business woman
She told me her only problem was a
terrible fear of spiders*

*This fear had existed for a long time
but was getting worse and was interfering with her life
If she spotted a spider in her house she had to run
outdoors and could not return until the exterminator had
sprayed and reassured her that all spiders were dead*

*In the first session I told her that we would begin some
behavioral work at a slow and easy pace*

*First I would assist her in learning how to relax
by using a "body scan" technique
beginning with her relaxing the muscles in her
right foot/leg and then the left foot/leg
Slowly and progressively she then moved
the relaxation process up the body to the top of her head*

*Next she turned her attention to quietening her mind
Then she moved on to learn the visualization process
She was instructed to use her imagination and
visualize herself in a transparent bubble
This was her "safe haven"
Here she would be safe and
could float from place to place*

*I told her to imagine floating over a beach gliding silently
near the ground so that she could even see insects –
including spiders – on the ground*

She was in complete control

If she felt herself becoming anxious she simply controlled her bubble to move higher and away from the spiders

*By moving the bubble back and forth
she was able to gain courage and self-confidence
She was in a safe place
She was in control
She no longer felt threatened
She was not anxious even when
she was a short distance from the spiders*

*After practicing this visualization process for several sessions she moved on to the next phase of the de-sensitization process
Here she again did her body scan to become relaxed*

*Then we both sat on the floor
I gave her a fly swat and I had one as well
I demonstrated for her how to swat imaginary bugs
with vigor and at the same time to shout "Gotcha"
as we hit the floor with our fly swats
(This looks and sounds silly but it introduces
a playful attitude into a serious process)*

*Again we practiced this behavior long enough for her
to feel comfortable in making these motor moves*

*In our next session again we sat on the floor with
our fly swats beating on the floor at the imaginary bugs*

But then we went on to the next level

*I placed several plastic spiders on the floor
at some distance from her*

*When she felt ready I asked her to slowly and gradually
move closer to the fake spiders – all the while
swatting the floor and shouting "Gotcha"*

*Finally she was close enough to the spiders that she was
able to swat one and then another
All the while I was cheering her on with
encouraging words –"You can do it" – "Keep it going"
And she did*

*We remained at this level for several sessions
until she was completely comfortable – even bored*

*And then we went to the final phase –
returning to the use of imagination/visualization
only this time she was to visualize that
she was in a room with a live spider
and she was to stay at a distance from the spider until
she felt comfortable and
then slowly she was to move closer to it*

*If at any time she felt herself becoming anxious
she was to back off – focus on her breathing –
become comfortable –
and re-approach the imaginary spider
After several trials she got close enough and then
Wham – she swatted it – shouting "Gotcha"*

That was it
She looked at me – smiled – and said "I can do it"

We had no more sessions
Later she called to say that in real life
she had been able to kill a spider –
even shouting "Gotcha" as she swatted it

∞

My Spiritual Gourd

This labyrinth gourd reflects my own spiritual journey

*The definition of the ancient word "labyrinth"
is any inextricable or bewildering state of things*

Certainly my spiritual journey is that

*The labyrinth deceives us
First we think we are getting closer to our goal
Then suddenly – sometimes even wildly –
we discover we are not even close
With one turn of the bend
we find ourselves far from our center*

*Also note the pathways – sometimes wide enough
to walk in comfortably – but then again
so narrow we can barely squeeze through –
requiring some effort to traverse our path*

*The barriers and resistances blocking our way
cause the weary to fall by the wayside
but they also challenge us
They demand that we put forth
the best that lies within us*

*Now observe the body of the gourd –
note in particular the defects
Some were with the gourd from the beginning
Others resulted from the wear and tear of growing
Certainly no one would talk of this gourd as being perfect*

*But who wants perfection
when wholeness is so much better*

*All in all there is something loveable about this gourd
After all it did teach me patience –
and certainly I have been lacking in that*

*And how about endurance
In carving the gourd I encountered
frustration after frustration and yet I endured
I stayed with the task even when I felt so helpless*

*Something from within the gourd
reminded me of my goal
Something called forth the best within me
And when that didn't seem to be enough
the gourd quietly forgave me
and I journeyed on*

∞

Reply from the Thou

*As I lay there in the darkness
tears flowed freely down my cheeks*

*Mine were not tears of sadness
Mine were tears of joy – of renewal
I felt my burdens lifted – I felt my pain relieved*

A moment to remember – a moment to cherish

*I could not explain this moment
It certainly was not created by my actions
I simply surrendered – I simply let go*

Then who did create this moment – I asked

*From the silence within the reply came
"It is from me Precious One -
the Thou who knew you from the beginning -
the Thou who will be with you forever"*

*My lips spoke not a word but my heart answered loudly
"Thank you Blessed One –
Thy Presence is mine to cherish"*

∞

George W. Barnard M.D.

The Perfect Hostess

*I first met Ms R as a referral from
the Gastro-Intestinal (GI) Department
She was a 67 year old woman who had developed
a severe problem with swallowing
and as a result had lost a considerable amount of weight*

*Her GI physician had been concerned that
she might have a malignancy
but her workup had been negative so
they referred her to me for a psychiatric evaluation*

*She denied having any emotional problems and
specifically denied any depressive symptoms
She told me that she was married to a man who had
retired from the diplomatic service during the past year
and had come to the university for graduate study*

*They never had children and she had spent
most of her adult life entertaining guests
associated with her husband's work*

*Now that he was a student
she no longer was expected to entertain guests
Although she spoke as though
she was relieved to no longer have these duties
the quality of her voice indicated to me that
her role as a hostess had been of
great significance to her*

*Since she showed no overt signs of depression –
refused to try any anti-depressive medication –
and was reluctant to engage in any exploratory
psychotherapy – I decided to establish a
relationship with her on grounds where
she might be more comfortable and in which
we could also grapple with the swallowing problem*

*I asked her if she would be willing to prepare
a lunch for us and bring it in a picnic basket
each time she came to see me*

*She was delighted to do this and
each week we would sit in my office
and eat the meal she had prepared*

*During this time she was the perfect hostess
and her personality was a lot more outgoing
She – not I – was in control of the situation*

*I made no attempt to do any "psychiatric talk"
Rather I was her guest and we engaged
strictly in "social talk"*

*At first she ate very little but within a short time
she was able to swallow without any problem and
was able to eat a normal amount of food*

*During this time her ability to trust me increased and
she gradually gave up her denial and
began to talk more openly about her
great sense of loneliness*

George W. Barnard M.D.

*Her husband was away much of the time and
she didn't know anyone in the neighborhood*

*But the big issue was her loss of being of importance to
others now that she no longer functioned as
the hostess and entertained guests*

*She had never discussed this with her husband
He had no idea of the importance it was to her
She could see that this was a problem that concerned
both her and her husband and agreed to ask him to come
in so the three of us could discuss it*

*Her husband was quite willing to come and was a lot
more agreeable to participate than she
had imagined he would be*

*He too missed entertaining guests and was open
to her suggestion that they begin to invite some of his
fellow students over weekly for drinks and snacks
as they got to know each other*

*Within weeks her "swallowing problem" had completely
disappeared and she was back to her old self*

∞

Seeking the Watering Hole

*She staggered from the doctor's office
with those deadly words
still echoing loudly in her head
"Your tumor is cancerous – it's inoperable
Your tumor is cancerous – it's inoperable"*

*It seemed she was trapped in a time warp
Time desperately frozen in that very moment
refusing to go forward*

*When time did start again
it was accompanied by waves of terror – then –
Nausea – Dizziness – Vomiting*

*Vomiting as never before
Collapsing her to her knees
There she felt more stable
Perhaps because the position
was associated with prayer*

*And pray she did
Asking for strength – for guidance*

*Her guides were with her
Reassuring – comforting*

*Slowly her mind settled
Once again able to think*

George W. Barnard M.D.

*Once again able to remember
the rest of her doctor's words
"You have other options –
Chemotherapy – Radiation"*

But would they help

*"Cure – No
Prolong life – Yes"*

*She knew the decision was hers
She also knew it would not be made today*

*Today was for dealing with basic survival issues
Today was for breathing deeply –
for becoming calm – centered
Time to remove panic – fear
Time for courage*

She knew her big battle was ahead – she must prepare

*As animals seek the water holes at dawn
to replenish their bodies –
so now she goes inward with meditation
to nourish her Soul –
to replenish her Body –
to renew her Spirit*

∞

Suffering Is Part of Isness

*At times I think I am a slow learner
At other times I know I am*

*I keep thinking that on my spiritual journey
I should reach a point where I no longer suffer
I so want to be free of suffering –
I think if I work hard enough
I can be free of it*

*Then I realize – that can never be
Suffering is part of life – I can never escape it
Well then if I can't escape it how can I learn to accept it*

*First I ask myself why do I want to avoid it so much
The answer comes back
Because suffering is painful*

*But when I look more deeply
I see that my fear is a bigger problem
I fear suffering because suffering – not me – is in control*

*Again I see the presence of Ego trying to control –
trying to be in charge*

*What if I try a different approach
As Observer-Witness Self I simply watch
I step aside – become detached
I simply let my suffering be –
I let my fears be
I observe them – without trying to change them
As I observe I realize I am not alone*

George W. Barnard M.D.

*Divine Self is with me –
to comfort me – to reassure me*

*Also as I observe I realize my suffering – my fears –
are not steady states –
they fluctuate – they vary
sometimes strong – sometimes weak
As I become less fearful of my dukha – my suffering
I can approach it – I can dialogue with it*

*What does it want of me
What does it want to teach me – teach me about myself*

*When I approach it in this manner
I see that my suffering is sacred –
part of the sacred whole*

*Through my suffering I learn about the universe
but more importantly I learn about me –
about my relationship to the Other -
about my relationship to the Divine*

*When experienced with this understanding
suffering and I are part of the sacred whole*

We are part of the Isness

∞

The Inner Crucible

*I was the one with a heart bound
tightly with bands of steel*

*Who would be the blow torch to set me free
so that I could feel love and compassion*

*I was the one who groped about
in my cave of darkness and ignorance*

*Who would be the bright lantern of wisdom
that guided me to light and understanding*

*I was the one whose mind was caught in a whirlwind
of constant chatter so that I flitted from topic to topic*

*Who would be the windmill that guided my mind
so that I could concentrate deeply*

*I was the one who was caught in the mud pit of greed
Who would be my hip boots so that I could
walk onto the solid ground of generosity*

*I was the one whose Soul was parched
by the heat of fear and anger*

*Who would be the soothing stream of water
in which I could bathe so that my vitality was restored
and once again I felt joy and gladness*

*I was the one whose spiritual vision was blurred
as to where I was going and why*

George W. Barnard M.D.

*Who would be the one to be my glasses
to make my vision clear and in accord
with my Soul's desire*

*I was the one who was totally encased
in my cocoon of Egotism*

*Who would be the gardener that freed my butterfly
so that I could spread my wings of kindness to others*

*I searched and searched to find one
who might accomplish this difficult task but to no avail*

It was then I decided I must do it alone

*It was then that I went within to meet
my natural sources of healing and restoration*

*Whether I was sick in Body – Mind – Soul – Spirit
It was here that I found my source of relief
It was here I found my freedom*

*It was here I learned how I could
respond skillfully to painful emotions*

It was here I learned who I am and who I may become

*It was here that I achieved my moksha –
my spiritual enlightenment*

I found that here isn't so bad after all

∞

Unlocking Life's Secrets

Longing for a Life that Matters

She had walked some distance to get to the well

*As she approached she noticed a stranger sitting nearby
Immediately she could tell that he was not one of them*

"Can I get a drink of water from you?" he asked

*"Why are you talking to me?" she responded
"I am a Samaritan – not a Jew as are you
Jews have nothing to do with us Samaritans
so why do you ask of me for a drink"*

*"I am thirsty" Jesus said
"But I also have something to offer you
If you drink of this water your thirst will return
but I offer you 'living water'
If you drink of this water
your inner thirst will not return"*

*She laughed and said
"You are probably pulling my leg
but if not give me some of that magic liquid"*

*Jesus responded
"It is not magic –
you speak of material reality –
I speak of spiritual reality
Go and get your husband
I will tell both of you of this living water"*

"I have no husband" she said

George W. Barnard M.D.

*"I know" Jesus said "You have had five husbands
and are not married to the man you live with"*

*"Sir are you some kind of guru –
how do you know of me?"*

*At that moment many painful memories flashed by her
She recalled with much pain
all the abusive relationships she had been in
"How do you know me so well?"*

*"I know your spirit" Jesus said
"I know that deep within you strive for purpose –
I know that your Soul searches for meaning to your life"*

*She responded "Indeed my Soul is dry –
my Soul longs for a life that matters –
my Soul longs to be healed"
Then she gave Jesus the drink he had requested*

*In turn Jesus gently touched her forehead
"Now go in peace" he said*

*The woman thanked him
She took her water jars and returned to her village
with her face beaming with joy
as she told everyone of the encounter*

*"Come – you must meet this unique man" she exclaimed
"He offers us so much
If only we open our hearts so that we can hear"*

∞

The Re-Awakening

*When I first met Jim – a 72 year old retired minister –
he was sitting hunched over in a chair in his room
at our psychiatric in-patient unit*

*He was staring straight ahead – when I introduced
myself he never acknowledged my presence
He simply continued to stare straight ahead
with a very sad look on his face*

*At first he did not speak so I remained by his side
in silence for a few minutes
I then placed my hand on his shoulder and the
conversation went something like this*

*"Reverend P – I understand that your doctor sent
you to us because you have had a very bad depression"*

"Yes" he replied in a very soft voice

"Can you tell me something about it?" I asked

*"It is too horrible to talk about" he said as tears
began to flow silently down his face*

*"Your wife told me that you have talked of
wanting to kill yourself" I said*

*"Yes I thought it was the only way out" he replied
"My thoughts were so horrible – so sinful –
I thought I needed to die
I wanted to bash my brains out"
Gradually his story emerged*

George W. Barnard M.D.

*During the six months prior to his admission to our
hospital he had become more depressed and had been
treated in his community hospital but had not improved*

*He had lost weight – had very little sleep –
and had no desire to live because of one obsessive thought
that he ruminated about night and day*

*The obsessive painful thought that
he described as being horrible/sinful was
"Cornhole Jesus"*

*For a minister who had spent his entire career
preaching about a loving God - to have this sexually
derogatory and aggressive thought
was more than he could tolerate*

*On the psychiatric unit Jim was always alone
He never initiated conversation and if he was spoken to
he replied in very short sentences
His speech was so soft it was hard to hear
He spoke in a monotone without any changes in pitch*

*His facial muscle tone was bland and
he avoided eye contact with others
He sat motionless in his chair for long periods of time just
staring into space as though he were a
frightened animal afraid to move*

*It was obvious that in his deep depression
he had shut down many components of who he was
All in all it was as though his entire body-mind-spirit
was in an immobile sleep-like mode*

Unlocking Life's Secrets

*Our first goal then was to show Jim that it was
safe to become reawakened – safe to become alive again*

*(In retrospect our initial task could be seen as a
re-activation of his Sympathetic Nervous System without
overly frightening him so that there was less dominance
by the Ancient Unmyelinated Vagal system*

*Once he was unstuck from this Ancient level then he
could return to the most recent Modern Myelinated
Vagal system as described by Stephen Porges
in his book "The Polyvagal Theory")*

*The initial work between Jim and me was to
take place in a room barren of furniture –
called "the play room" by some and
"the mud room" by others
Both of us wore casual clothes that could
easily be washed because they were going
to get dirty each time we met*

*Our working "tools" were clay-water –
a medicine ball – and 2 bongo drums*

*In our first session together the aim was for Jim
to become more aware of what was going on in his body*

*We began with some breathing exercises focusing on Jim
learning deep abdominal breathing*

*At first his breaths were shallow but in a short time
he was able to learn the technique of inhaling deeply –
pausing – and then gradually exhaling*

George W. Barnard M.D.

*During this time I asked Jim to notice how natural it was
to "take in" a breath and "let go" of a breath*

*Then I asked him to become aware of how natural it is
to do the same with our thoughts –
we "have" a thought and we "let go" of a thought*

*It will take time and practice but
the "letting go" process can be learned
We then turned to throwing the medicine ball
back and forth to each other*

*At first in silence I threw the ball very gently and slowly
Jim was able to follow in kind*

*Then gradually I increased the force and speed
but Jim continued to throw with his gentle force*

*Even when I encouraged him to throw the ball harder –
at first he had difficulty doing so*

*With my continuing to role model
how I wanted him to do it
gradually he was able to increase the force and speed*

*All the time I was cheering him on
I kept asking for more and more and he delivered*

*Next as I demonstrated what I wanted him to do
I asked him to shout "Ho!" each time he threw the ball*

*He attempted to do so but his shouts were not very loud
and his throws were less forceful than before*

Unlocking Life's Secrets

*With encouragement he was able to increase
the loudness of his shouts and the force of his throws*

*But then when I asked him to shout
"No!" instead of "Ho!"
he once again dropped both his level of shouts
and his degree of force while throwing the ball*

*I called his attention to this process so that
he would be more aware of how
his body was reacting as we changed
the level of complexity of his behavior*

*During each of our sessions together I attempted to
engage him in activities that would require
not only activation of his motor or muscular system
but in this safe environment would also
expand his emotional and social behavioral abilities*

*For instance in one exercise we would stand
in front of each other and I would push on his shoulder
hard enough to cause his body to move easily
because he stood with his feet close together
and therefore his base of stability was not strong*

*But then I showed him how to broaden his base
so that I could not move him*

*This was done to make him aware that
he could make changes in his body
that would assist his defensive stance as needed*

George W. Barnard M.D.

*Resisting my attempt to move him
automatically took him out of his passive role
and put him in an active-assertive role –
thereby activating his Sympathetic Nervous System*

*I not only wanted to re-awaken the large muscles
I also wanted to re-awaken the muscles in Jim's
face – neck – throat and larynx
so I stood in front of him and
role-modeled behaviors I wanted from him*

*I puffed out my cheeks – made all kinds of grimaces –
snarled – growled – fluttered my lips –
even stuck out my tongue – in order to get
the feel of play stimulated in Jim*

*I asked Jim to mirror back to me each of these behaviors
and as with the large muscles at first
his attempts were feeble but with encouragement he kept
at it until he was able to show strong responses*

*All the time that Jim was engaged in
making his motor reactions
I was monitoring his facial and eye movements
to give me non-verbal indication
of how he was reacting emotionally*

*I felt that this was necessary because early in the process
he might not be aware of how he was feeling
but at a non-conscious level his body could and did
communicate his emotional reactions*

*In many ways this is like the attunement that is
necessary between mother and infant –
much of the communication is done at
this non-verbal level*

*Also as it is with mother and infant
the concept of play is very important
in order to lighten the atmosphere and
communicate that this is a safe/secure environment*

*We can engage in behaviors that are new and that are
preparing the patient for later phases of the
growth/maturation process*

*The intent is not to harm the individual but to assist
him/her in the healing process*

*Participating in this type of body work can be
perceived as threatening by some patients and
it is essential that the therapist transmit a
caring/respectful attitude for the patient at all times*

*Since this body work approach calls for a certain degree of
physical contact between therapist and patient that is not
present in the usual social engagements
it is mandatory that the therapist at no time do anything
that can be perceived as being sexually provocative*

*There must be a crystal clear understanding that
therapist/patient boundaries should not be crossed
The therapist carries the responsibility
to set these boundaries*

George W. Barnard M.D.

*During Jim's course of therapy an interesting
event related to perception occurred*

*One day Jim told me that his wife was curious about
what was taking place in his therapy and he would like to
have her come in for one of his treatment sessions
I agreed and Mrs P came*

*She was a bit uptight throughout the session but became
distraught at one point as Jim and I were playing the
bongo drums and making weird-sounding animal noises*

*She said that she was going to talk with
the hospital director*

*At that point Jim's back stiffened
and in a very firm voice he said
"You will not do that!
My doctor is helping me and I am getting better"*

*This was a turning point in the course of his therapy
Indeed the tiger had awakened*

*After this point he improved rapidly
Everything about him was quite a bit different
He walked erect
He made eye contact as he spoke
and he talked with self-confidence
His depression improved dramatically
His obsessive thinking occurred only occasionally
and he more easily engaged in conversation with others*

*Lessons learned in the "play room" were continued with
other members of the treatment team working with Jim*

*The nursing staff engaged him in games in which he
could continue to show his inner strength and courage*

*The occupational therapist used finger paints to assist
him in gaining additional skill in being loose and flexible*

*The hospital chaplain participated in some of the "play
room" sessions so that Jim could experience a fellow
minister engaging in some of the "playful" activities*

*For instance picture the three of us marching around the
room in a circle singing "Jesus loves me"
in a loud voice as we in rhythm slapped each other
on the back with some vigor*

*All in all there was a concerted attempt made for
Jim to carry his newfound assertive abilities into the
world reality outside the hospital –
truly a re-socialization process*

*As he was being discharged for follow-up with
his local psychiatrist he grinned at me and said
"You know Doc – we did have fun! Thanks!
You and your team helped me regain my life"*

∞

George W. Barnard M.D.

The Aftermath of Sexual Assault

*I first met Mae about 50 years ago
when she was 27 years old*

*She had been admitted to our psychiatric unit
because of debilitating anxiety and depression –
and a long history of urinary retention*

*Her problems began at age 12 after she was raped
by a 50 year old neighbor who threatened
to kill her if she revealed that he raped her*

*Almost immediately following the rape
she was unable to void – developed fever –
and was unable to get out of bed*

*She was catheterized a number of times
and then had an indwelling catheter placed*

*Later this was followed by a cystostomy
with a urinary sac for a year
and then she was able to void for several years*

*Her inability to void began again at age 18
after she had intercourse
with a boyfriend and became pregnant*

*She required intermittent catheterizations during the
pregnancy and following the delivery
for the next several years*

*At age 25 she began dating a man and
told him about the illegitimate child*

*He beat her severely on several occasions and
threatened to reveal her secret unless she married him*

*He made several sexual advances to her that led
to a complete urinary retention
requiring an indwelling catheter*

*She did marry this man and stayed with him
for several months during which time he
inflicted sadistic punishments on her
After she left him she was in fear because of his threats*

*For the next several years she required intermittent
catheterizations but otherwise did well*

*At age 26 she met a man she felt comfortable with
and they married*

*Soon after the marriage her urinary symptoms worsened
and she was hospitalized on several occasions and
had genitourinary surgery but had no relief*

*She became highly anxious and severely depressed
She was treated with electroconvulsive
therapy without relief*

*Following several months of unsuccessful
outpatient psychotherapy she was admitted to our
psychiatric hospital for evaluation and treatment*

*Perhaps the best way to describe Mae is that she looked
and acted like a very frightened child-like young woman
who at times would become agitated and claw at her face*

*She was preoccupied with feelings of inadequacy
as a wife and as a mother as well as with
her chronic urinary retention problems*

*The urologist impression was that she had
an acquired sensory neurogenic bladder*

*At that time Post Traumatic Stress Disorder (PTSD) was
not part of our official diagnostic labels
but we did believe that she had undergone a
severe traumatic experience with the rape
causing her subsequent urinary retention problems*

*Our speculation was that she had an overactive
Sympathetic activation of the bladder-sphincter system*

*The main issue then was how to decrease the Sympathetic
dominance so that her bladder could
receive a more normal activation from the
Sympathetic Nervous System so that the
Parasympathetic Nervous System could do its job*

*From my previous research in stress at the Aerospace
Medical Research Laboratory we had found that often
when a stressor is presented there is an initial
Sympathetic response during the anticipatory and stress
phases but during the recovery phase there is a
heightened or prolonged Parasympathetic response*

*We explained the plan to assist her in relearning how to
relax and empty her bladder and she agreed to try it*

*In order to reaffirm her sense of safety a nurse remained
with her as she sat on a commode in an adjoining room*

*Electrodes were attached to her legs so that
she could receive an ongoing electrical stimulus
from a stimulator for about 60 seconds*

*We asked her to let us know when the pain level
became almost intolerable so that the stimulus could
immediately be terminated at that point*

*She was tense with the first trial but with the
second attempt she relaxed sufficiently so that
she was able to void 600 ml spontaneously*

*This technique was done three times a day
but within several days she was given control of the
stimulus and successfully carried out
the procedure herself and was able to void*

*In the next phase the patient learned to shout "NO"
when she wished for the self-administered pain to stop
and to terminate the electrical stimulus
After a short time of using this paired conditioning
procedure she was able to relax and void
by simply saying "NO"*

*Once the patient had mastered regaining voluntary
control of her bladder the emphasis of the therapy shifted
so that she could learn and master self-assertive behaviors
at an interpersonal level –
first with staff and other patients and
then gradually with family members*

George W. Barnard M.D.

*Within one month she was entirely free of the urinary
retention problems and there was no subsequent relapse
It took her several more months of intense treatment
to learn to effectively deal with family
members without becoming anxious*

*She regained her self-confidence as a wife and mother –
was able to lose her fear of men –
became comfortable with sex –
and was able to experience orgasms
during intercourse with her husband*

*She learned to drive – got her license
and became active in community work*

*On follow-up several years later she appeared happy
and expressed confidence in herself
She was optimistic about her life in the future*

*In the nearly fifty years since this patient was treated
much has been learned about the brain
and the effect of rape trauma on the victim*

*Clearly the traumatic rape experience highly activated the
Amygdala and the Hypothalamic Pituitary Adrenal Axis
with an outpouring of the stress hormones
Cortisol and Adrenaline so that she remained
in a chronic state of stress*

*(In retrospect – using the evolutionary model which
Stephen Porges discusses in his book "The Polyvagal
Theory" – we could say that she was constantly
functioning in the Sympathetic mode*

In a safe setting we helped her to regain self-regulatory control so that she was able to let go of old maladaptive ways and function in a healthy – productive lifestyle)

∞

Note: My colleagues and I published this case report in an article entitled "The Treatment of Urinary Retention by Aversive Stimulus Cessation and Assertive Training" in Behavior Research and Therapy Volume 4, Pages 232-236. England: Pergamon, 1966.

George W. Barnard M.D.

Unfolding From Being

*I stood on the beach
and watched the waves roll in*

*First a small – even tiny wave
Then it unfolded into a gigantic one
only then to fold into the ocean again
Or was it ever anything but ocean*

And so it is with all of life

*We unfold from Being
and for a while may feel – and even act –
as though we are separate –
like the wave*

*We give it a name –
Ego
Sometimes becoming
Inflated Ego*

*But always folding
back into Being*

*Wouldn't it be nice to realize
We are Being
all the time*

*Tat Tvam Asi
Thou Art That*

∞

Unnamed Woman

She stood there in silence
She stood there in awe
She had heard so much of this One

But could it be real
Could he offer her hope
Could he offer her release
Release from her suffering

Twelve long years of suffering
Twelve long years of shame
Twelve long years of shunning

Now – just perhaps now – there was hope

She had tried so many routes for healing
But all had failed

Why should it be different this time
Why should she hope for relief
But hope she did

No not hope – a better name was trust
Trust in a force greater than she
Trust in a healing force

But how to make it available
How to make it available for her

She was considered unclean
She was considered unworthy

George W. Barnard M.D.

*For her even to touch another
was to make that one also unclean*

*What were her options
She could open her heart
She could become receptive
Receptive for healing forces
Receptive for redeeming forces*

And so she did

*Perhaps she could also touch his garment
She could do this and not be noticed
And so she did*

She lovingly touched his coat

*There was mingling of Soul with Soul
There was union of grace with trust*

*Immediately her hemorrhaging stopped
Her body felt healed*

*But her touch had not gone unnoticed
The One who had been touched knew it
He knew it because he felt drained
Drained of his prana –
his healing energy*

*His eyes searched for the source of his loss
The woman saw him and trembled in fear
She knew she was the recipient of his gaze*

She was the one to receive his energy
What was she to do
Run or come forth and confess
She chose the latter

She came forth and told her story
She was received with compassion

Not only did he accept her
He acknowledged her power

Your faith has made you well
Your trust has made you whole

In your wholeness – Worthy One –
Go in peace

∞

George W. Barnard M.D.

You Are Accepted

Since early childhood Zach felt rejected

*He was born premature
and later his growth was delayed
Being short in stature was a real handicap
None of the guys wanted him on their team*

*Being uncoordinated didn't help
It seemed his limbs had ideas of their own*

*Since he was short the girls also shied away
Feeling unaccepted by both sexes he began to withdraw*

*More and more he preferred
being alone and in his head
He was a good student and
that offered some compensation*

*When alone with his thoughts he was safe
For Zach thoughts were safer than feelings*

*He found learning gave him power and security
Knowledge also helped him to get a well-paying job
He became a rich but despised tax collector
He was hated and rejected but well-paid*

*Still deep within there was a longing for acceptance
It was a secret longing but still a longing*

*Then he heard the news
A famous rabbi was coming to town
The throngs poured out to see him*

Unlocking Life's Secrets

Even Zach was curious

He wanted to get a glimpse of the master
He tried but because of his shortness
he couldn't see the rabbi
so he climbed a sycamore tree

Just then the rabbi was passing by
A movement of the branches
must have caught his eye

Jesus stopped beneath the tree and called out
"Zach, come down!
I wish to eat with you today"

Zach was stunned
As he climbed down the tree he stammered
"How could you know my name?"

Zach's heart opened with joy
as the master simply opened his arms
and answered his question with a welcoming smile

This was a moment of spiritual transformation for Zach
"Never in my life have I felt so accepted" he exclaimed

No longer did he feel like an outcast
No longer was his short stature an issue

"My heart has been healed
by your love and acceptance"
he shouted with joy

*"From this day forth I will freely share
both myself and my wealth with the poor
For those I have overcharged
I will give back four times the amount"*

*Jesus responded
"Today you have obtained freedom from your lesser-self
Today you begin the spiritual journey
for which you have longed*

*This is the journey of letting go and of acceptance
You let go of the false – the unreal
You accept the true – the real"*

∞

Who Benefits from Forgiveness?

*From early childhood we are taught that
we should forgive those who wrong us*

*Those who tell us this make it sound as though
in some way we are relieving the wrongdoer of a burden*

*But if we look at it carefully
it is we the forgivers who are benefited*

*It is our Souls that are relieved of a heavy burden
It is in the process of forgiveness that we let go*

*We let go of the negative emotions
anger – hatred – resentment – bitterness
that if left on their own will dry up our Souls
like the sun dries plums and turns them into prunes*

*If we keep our negative emotions
then we deny ourselves of something precious
We deny ourselves the joy
of experiencing our positive emotions
love – pleasure – joy – happiness – peace*

*But perhaps an even greater benefit in letting go
of our hatred – our resentment – our bitterness
is that when we forgive the wrongdoer
we deny him/her the ability to have power over us –
deny him/her the ability to control us*

*If we hold onto our negative emotions then
we are still permitting the wrongdoer
to have power/control over us whether we like it or not*

*If we retain the negative emotions generated
during our encounter with the wrongdoer
we are still maintaining our bodies in a fight mode*

*We are still churning out the stress hormones –
Cortisol and Adrenaline
These are helpful hormones for short term battles
but if generated over prolonged periods of time
they function as poisons not only for our Souls
but also for our bodies*

*We may send out energy signals of forgiveness
to a wrongdoer but we can't control
whether the forgiveness is accepted or rejected*

*If accepted the forgiveness can have a
transforming effect on the wrongdoer
but if our forgiveness is rejected by the wrongdoer
it is powerless to facilitate any changes in him/her*

*The important variable in the transformation of the
wrongdoer is whether or not the heart of
the wrongdoer is open/receptive or closed/rejecting*

*But regardless of what actions the wrongdoer takes
We benefit greatly by being a forgiver*

It is our choice

∞

Homecoming

*If I wish to go on an evolutionary adventure
then I enter the numinous place of my being
Here I will not be confined by limitations of time or space*

*Whether I am in the realm of light or particle
I have paradoxical flexibility to behave like
separate particles and also like waves*

*It is here I can escape the boundaries of Ego
and satisfy my longing to experience the presence of God*

*I participate in a direct relationship
My Divine Self merges with Divine Spirit*

*Enjoying Oneness – Being –
Nothingness – Limitlessness
Polarities synthesized –
Dualities transcended*

*Emerging from the union with Primordial Energy
I am transformed – enriched – rejuvenated
I have become aware of my Yehidah endowment*

*My highest being
connected to the Divine*

Homecoming in its truest sense

∞

George W. Barnard M.D.

With Forgiveness Comes Relief

As I go through life certain patterns reemerge
Reemerge again and again
The pattern of offending the Other – You

I try not to do so but I do
Sometimes I deny it
Sometimes I admit it

But either way that old demon guilt still
hangs onto me with a deadly hold

I feel constricted like a squeezed balloon
The air in my lungs barely moves
I feel like a prisoner in my own body

How do I get relief
How do I set myself free

First I take responsibility for my actions
I acknowledge I wounded your Soul –
intentionally or not

Then I ask your forgiveness
If it comes I feel calmness
But if you withhold forgiveness – then what

Then comes my real hurdle
Whether I have wronged you – or God
I will never have peace
until I forgive myself

*Then I remember what Jesus said about
the Kingdom of God*

*In this Kingdom forgiveness is not necessary
God accepts us as we are – deserving or not*

This gives me hope

If God accepts me – maybe I can accept me

∞

Chapter 4: Link to the Divine

Chit-Sat-Ananda/Awareness-Being-Bliss

*As I begin a new day – today –
I have a choice – I ask myself
What are my intentions*

*Shall I experience my real essence or
shall I continue to deprive myself of the real me*

*Do I dare encounter this inner sacred being
Do I deserve to be so blessed
Shall I open my heart to the truth of reality*

*Indeed there is a materialistic me
But equally important there also is a spiritual me*

*This concept cannot be processed
with the left hemisphere of my brain
It handles information linearly and rationally*

*This spiritual information must be handled by
the right hemisphere of the brain
which grasps concepts holistically and intuitively*

*Therefore let my right hemisphere
guide me on my spiritual journey*

*Let my imaginative mind guide me through images
Images that speak not to my senses but
to my Soul – to my Spirit*

In a Meditative State
I let my ordinary sense of things about me fade
so that I may experience only the
joy of the deep silence that is within

First Chit – awareness
I go inward to my sacred space
I become aware of Divine Self

This is my Sat – my being

Then as Divine Self I experience
the presence of God/dess – the Divine Spirit

This is something I have longed for
Now I settle back and experience this inner joy

I desire and am desired
I love and am loved
I let my tears of joy and ecstasy flow as
I rejoice in the presence of the Divine

I let my heart – my mind – and my Soul
be receptive to this Presence

I let my Divine Self soak up this grace of renewal

I let my Divine Self be bathed in
the love of Divine Spirit so that
Divine Self may blossom in love for itself

As I experience the merger of this love
of Divine Self and that of Divine Spirit
I realize that this is Ananda – this is bliss

George W. Barnard M.D.

*While in this blissful state I allow my
imaginative mind to go beyond language*

*I open myself to its healing forces so that they may
penetrate every cell of my body*

In deep internal silence I pause and savor this moment

*Then as I emerge again
from a Meditative State
I feel refreshed –
I feel rejuvenated –
I feel whole*

∞

essence is Essence

*Often I have wondered what my Soul was
before I was born –
or what it will be after I die*

*Perhaps the mystery becomes solved
when I realize that my Soul is essence -
which is part of Essence*

*Thus my Soul
never was – is not – never will be –
separate essence*

Because essence is Essence

∞

George W. Barnard M.D.

Feast at the Master's Table

I savor my Kenosis – my letting go
Surrendering all those things
that keep me from experiencing God's Love

So I strive to let go of:
The chronic Anxieties and Fears of the unknown
that I cling to as if they were precious metals
even though they devour my composure

The Ego-centeredness that keeps me
blown up like a stuffed turkey
insisting that my desires must be met

The Resentment that comes
when I don't get my way festers in my Soul
like a boil full of pus just about to burst –
spreading its poison onto all it touches

The Denial – the self-deception
that leads me around blindfolded
so I never see the truth of who I really am

And ah that ever present Desire to be in control
that causes me to struggle to dominate
or fight to prevent being dominated

Then I stop and reflect:
Fear of the unknown
Perceived Threats to the Ego – real or unreal – and
Sense of Loss of Control
All three are the primary factors that produce stress

Unlocking Life's Secrets

So what can I do

I can enter a Meditative State
I can use imagery and practice my inner skills
wherein I move to a higher state of being
and function at times as Observer-Witness Self and
at other times as Divine Self so that I possess new powers

As I do I empty myself of these internal demons
and their unnamed cousins too

Then I use more imagery so that I can
come and feast at the Master's table

God's table of Grace is always prepared –
filled with platters of positive attributes
Joy – Compassion – Love – Forgiveness – Acceptance

Here I find satiation for my ever present hunger –
the hunger that comes from fragmentation

I sample God's harvest of love
and depart being teleios – fully complete – whole
But knowing that tommorow
I may return hungry and need to feed again

∞

George W. Barnard M.D.

Finding Harmony in the Numinous

I have suffered in loneliness

I have trembled in fear

I have felt my Soul parched with hatred and cruelty

I have felt my back bend with guilt and shame

I have felt my heart heave with sadness and grief

I have been crippled by the deadly grip of anxiety

I have felt very fragmented

Yet I do not despair

*I desire – I hunger –
I seek to fulfill the deepest yearning of my existence –
for my Divine Self to be reunited
in harmony with Divine Spirit*

*My creative life force seeks to find the
Original Creative Life Force*

My being seeks Being

*Once again I want to be rejuvenated
by receiving the blessing of the Divine Spirit –
to be a recipient of Life's Renewal –
the mysterious gift of grace*

Unlocking Life's Secrets

To be bathed in this grace brings
my fragmented self to experience wholeness

When I experience the Divine Spirit as within
my Soul feels full

I feel the joy of unification with my
primordial source of energy

This fountain is internal and is the
source of my spiritual being

My experience of reality comes from my interior
where the Divine Spirit dwells

I sense the Divine Spirit not by reason
but by opening my heart to the presence of Being

My inner certainty comes from having
wrestled with turmoil – conflict – paradox

I have been in touch with the timeless – with the Eternal
I have experienced the Divine Spirit – thus I know Being

This contact with the numinous has gripped and taxed
my being – giving me the very meaning of life

My inward knowledge thereby is rooted in experience

Let the inner directing force of the Divine Spirit
continue to transform my Divine Self –
the voice of my Soul

∞

George W. Barnard M.D.

Getting Through to God

*Lately - no – really for some time –
I feel I have had a
hard time getting through to God*

Maybe I need to:

Listen to God

*Not with my ears
But with my tears*

See God

*Not with my eyes
But with my deeds*

Taste God

*Not with my mouth
But with my joy*

Touch God

*Not with my hand
But with my heart*

Smell God

*Not with my nose
But with my dreams*

∞

Giving Up My Blindness

*Sometimes I think that I suffer from blindness –
blindness not of the material world
but of the spiritual realm –
that mysterious reality wherein
God/dess is within me
and can be experienced by me
no matter what exists without*

*This means I can experience God/dess
not only in my moments of joy
but also in my times of sorrow*

*How can I realize that
I can access this Sacred One
in every moment – in every Now*

*God's revelations are ongoing –
available for me to partake of
if I am willing to give up my blindness
and permit my Soul to bathe in
the Beloved's healing grace –
to reconnect with the ground of my being*

*As I re-establish contact with the Divine Source
I feel part of the universal mosaic that
connects me to all Others
As Jesus said
We are all branches of one tree – the tree of Life*

∞

George W. Barnard M.D.

God Needs Me

*Can I tolerate a strange idea that
God needs me
as much as
I need God*

*Without me who would be a direct channel
of God's creative energy*

God is shrouded in mystery and so am I

*What would happen if I allowed myself
to feel the divine that exists within me*

*Would it change my image of Self
if I allowed the Divine Spirit
to be experienced within me*

*Would I then discard my barriers
and acknowledge the presence of Divine Self*

Let me be receptive both to change and to being

*Become aware of the wealth that exists within
and mine my ores with loving care*

Re-establish harmony with this source of energy

Permit myself to participate in divine evolution

∞

I – As Co-Creator

*In the beginning there was Ein Sof –
Endless Being – Total Nothingness*

*Then the Light became manifest into
this world of beings*

*And so it is with my Spirit
first experienced as a fragmented being*

*Gradually manifesting into what only
I – the co-creator – determines*

As I listen to the inner voice

As I see with the third eye

As I become receptive to my true essence

*As I discover my potentials – my unknown –
my unrealized – my inner sacred Self*

*Really as I accept my wholeness
with all its imperfections*

∞

George W. Barnard M.D.

Joyful Reunion

*Having become fully awakened –
my Soul longed for a merger with the Beloved*

*It was not a hostile takeover but a friendly reunion
of source with Source – of being with Being*

*The separation was long and painful
as I wandered here and there
my Soul feeling fragmented and torn by
encounters on my life's journey*

*Marked by a sense of
alienation – loneliness – despair –
I was torn by the demons of polarity*

*Yet as I struggled to balance
transcendence and immanence
there was always a glimmer of hope*

*Despite my suffering – my homesickness –
there remained a bedrock of expectation
that someday the relationship
between Divine Self and Divine Spirit
would result in a joyful reunion
of spirit with Spirit*

*What was in the beginning
now once again has become*

∞

Life Sparks

Even when I am in the deepest of depressions –
my dark night of being –
still there is with me
tiny Life Sparks

Yes a flicker here – one there –
to give me hope that light still exists

These life sparks carry primordial wisdom
of the Ancient Ones existing within me

Wisdom given to me by my ancestors
thousands – if not millions – years ago

This wisdom was passed on with each step
of the evolutionary ascent

In some mysterious way these Sparks link me
both with my past and my future
because in this numinous realm
all is linked together in a unified whole
by what is called Life Force by some and God by others

When I realize this in the core of my being
then in true humility I accept the understanding that
this awesome Numinous Life Force – not I – is in control
and that my task is to become open/receptive
and allow myself to be guided by
the Wisdom of the Numinous

∞

George W. Barnard M.D.

Finding the One

*Let me look inward and find the One to whom I may feel
completely loyal*

*It is this One in which my fragmented being can
once again feel whole*

It is this One that will unite my Soul

This One is my Center

*It is in this One that Ego finally permits
its narcissistic demands to melt into
something greater than itself
and reluctantly allows the
egotistic fires to be quietened*

*When I see the face of the One
I see the image of the Soul of God
and the image of my own Soul –
in reality they are only one*

*Once I accept this then I am able to love
in myself all that which I previously had detested*

*Then I am free to accept – to love –
all in the Other that
I previously detested*

The opposites are reunited – are accepted – are owned

∞

Motion of the Butterfly

*As a butterfly
I lift my wings
to and fro in the evening breeze*

*This gentle motion –
reflective of my Soul calling to God –
has repercussions that are felt eons away
because I have made contact with the Divine –
both within and without*

*I care for God – God cares for me
My desire calls to God – God's desire calls to me
I long for God's love – God longs for my love
I belong to God – God belongs to me
Hallelujah – Hallelujah*

∞

George W. Barnard M.D.

Realizing God's Presence

*Now that I have learned somewhat
to be more honest with myself –
to lower my Mask Self – my pretend self –
let's see if I can be more honest with God*

*Can I drop my fake being and
approach God just as I am*

*This is not easy – it takes skill –
it takes practice – it takes patience
But most of all it takes surrender –
surrender of Ego –
with all of its thinking and rationality -
with all of its defensiveness and desire to control*

*Surrender of my Judgmental Self
with all of its condemning harshness -
with all of its restrictions - inhibitions – limitations*

*Let's get specific about what kind of skills are needed
Skill to detach myself from my
usual state of being so
I may gain access to a Meditative State*

*I find myself a quiet place
where I won't be interrupted
I sit in a comfortable position
so I can remain still for 30 minutes*

*I close my eyes and direct my attention inward
I take several deep abdominal breaths and relax*

*I focus on my breathing
I inhale through my nose for 1-2 seconds*

*Inhaling activates my Sympathetic Nervous System
keeping me alert – but not over wired*

*I then exhale through my mouth for 1-2-3-4 seconds
Exhaling stimulates my
Parasympathetic Nervous System –
keeping me relaxed and receptive to be healed –
allowing my body to relax with each cycle*

*As I focus on my breathing
I do not try to block out thoughts –
I just detach myself from them*

*When thoughts continue to intrude
I just focus on inhaling and then exhaling twice as long*

*I keep remembering my goal to remain receptive to the
presence of God – the Divine Spirit*

*I find it helpful to remind myself
of my divine origin – my divine heritage
To make this step I stop monitoring my breath
Instead I silently say "Hum" with each inbreath
and "Suh" with each outbreath*

*Hum-Suh
I am Self*

*This is my wholeness – my sacred wholeness
I continue in this silent receptive state
for 20-30 minutes*

*Practice means I should do this daily
whether I am in the mood or not -
whether I want to or not*

*Practice is discipline
Practice especially if I become discouraged
I certainly have been in the past and
expect to be in the future*

*Gradually my skillfulness will show
I may then practice twice a day*

*Patience means it takes time
Patience means it takes forgiveness
Forgiveness of myself as I become impatient
Forgiveness of myself as I become so relaxed that
I dose off in a twilight state or fall asleep*

*Forgiveness of myself when my mind chatters
I simply return to repeating Hum-Suh
And once again focus on my quiet state
In my state of silence I relax*

*This journey to find God is not an active one
I simply relax and realize God's presence
The presence of the Divine Spirit is always with me*

*I need only to remove the barriers and
realize – experience – accept
that I am never separate from the Divine Spirit*

*Perhaps the biggest barrier is Ego –
it likes to be in control*

*But if I am to experience the presence of God
Ego must surrender to God
Ego must become subservient to God as it did to Self
It will resist because it fears surrendering*

*This surrendering to the Divine Spirit is a mystical state
If I become open – empty – receptive
If I permit - if I allow
then sometimes there is a merger
A merger of being with Being*

*This is a blessed state – a state of grace –
really a state of wholeness
After I emerge from this numinous state
I feel enriched – alive*

*I have been in contact with my basic goodness
I have experienced the healing power of love
I then let go of my desire to cling to this state of vital
being and become willing to experience
the presence of God's prana as it unfolds
in my everyday life with me and all of my warts*

My sadhana – my sacred journey – continues

∞

George W. Barnard M.D.

Say Hello to God

*Last night I imagined
that God strolled through the garden
and I got a glimpse – a faint image
of this numinous Being*

*Later I had a dream and
God appeared in a different form*

*This morning as I meditated
God's image appeared to me once again
but not as before*

*Then I realized
God is a many-faced being
because God is Being*

*So when I greet a friend
or even a stranger
I do so with a loving heart*

*It just may be the Beloved
with yet another face*

∞

Spirit Waiting for Me

When I am lonely and need a Friend
There's Spirit waiting for me

When I am suffering and need to be healed
There's Spirit waiting for me

When I have sinned and need to confess
There's Spirit waiting for me

When I am hungry and need to be fed
There's Spirit waiting for me

When I have done someone wrong
and need to be forgiven
There's Spirit waiting for me

When I am depressed and my spirit is low
There's Spirit waiting for me

When my heart needs someone to love
There's Spirit waiting for me

When I die and walk to the other side
There's Spirit waiting for me

Wait no more Spirit

Come take my Hand
Come take my Mind
Come take my Soul

I join with Thee

∞

George W. Barnard M.D.

The Empty Vessel that is Full

*I come and drink
from the fountain of life –
quenching the thirst of
my parched Soul*

My sense of emptiness is filled

*My hunger is satiated
by my encounter with Divine Spirit*

*In the presence of my Beloved
my heart opens –
becoming a vessel
that runneth over with love –
yet remaining empty
to receive the love
of this Holy One*

*The Unknown of the Unknown
suddenly becomes known*

*In this unity
there is no separateness*

∞

True Identity

How locked am I to the concept of my identity

Do I recall when I passed from boyhood to being a man

Do I treasure an identity based on Ego – on doing –
or one based on Soul - on being

Can I tap both
my masculine energy – my yang energy
and my feminine energy - my yin energy

Can I let my psyche become a transformer for my Soul
so I can experience my own true identity –
fire and air
earth and water

Can I let Ego undergo many deaths
so I may find the God within –
so I may find the Goddess within

In my aloneness
I come into awareness of my oneness
I reach a certainty of balance

∞

George W. Barnard M.D.

Loosen My Bond

*Can I free my Soul of the cord that binds it to my craving
This is what limits me – this keeps me grounded*

*When my Spirit wants to soar with the eagles –
to be reunited with the Tao
to unloose my bond
to shed the false belief
that says I am only a body
and only the external is real*

*I must look inside –
uncover – unfold –
awaken to my sacred identity
that I am a spiritual being*

*I am connected to the Great Being –
to the Tao – to the Beloved*

*If I dare accept who I truly am
I will find an end to my addictive hunger*

My homesickness will be no more

*I will be home
I will be connected*

*My life will have meaning
I will be whole*

∞

With Spirits Renewed

*As I sat by the oceanside
the sun descended into darkness
carrying with it my Soul
on its descent into the unconscious*

*Each returning in the early hours of dawn
with spirits renewed for yet another day*

*My unconscious never seems to sleep
It is always on the prowl –
seeking to find new ways to speak to me
if only I would listen*

*Sometimes this is hard because
I do not want to hear what is being said*

I cannot believe it is really me being discussed

*But then I remember that
one of my many defenses is denial
and this somehow helps me get past this denial barrier
and I listen – shema – with an open heart*

Why

*Because at my core I know that
I am indeed linked to the Divine and hence
I bask in that renewed spirit
fully knowing that
I am well loved*

∞

George W. Barnard M.D.

You Are Not Alone

*We know that right now
you are going through a rough time*

But we want you to know that you are not alone

*Many friends – and count us among them –
have you in their thoughts and prayers*

*Have you ever seen a picture of a group of
penguins huddled together in a winter storm
This is the way they survive
the challenge of the bitter cold*

*In a similar way your friends
now surround you with their love
to help you keep strong in your challenging time*

*Even in your darkest moments
just remember that you are not alone*

*You may ask "Why am I not alone –
I certainly feel alone"
This is not to deny that you feel alone and also afraid*

*Still there are powerful voices
Voices from the heart encouraging you on*

*Pause for a moment –
Become still – become silent
and listen – shema*

*As you listen see if you can
hear the reassuring words of Jesus*

Fear not for I am with you

*Let these healing words from the Divine Spirit
speak personally to your Soul*

*Take in several deep breaths and
feel connected to the eternal*

Indeed you are not alone

∞

Chapter 5: Brain and Evolution

Being Human

*Do you have any idea of how many
neurons our brains have*

*Rick Hanson and Richard Mendias in their book
"Buddha's Brain" report that
we have over 100 billion
That is 100 followed by 9 zeros*

*But hold on – each neuron is estimated
to have 5,000 connections
So the total communication network is
500,000,000,000,000
Now that is a large number*

Why so many

Well the answer may surprise you – or maybe not

*Scientists think that we have this large number of
neurons in order to enable us to solve more complex
problems – especially those involved with being human
and communicating with one another*

*According to Louis Cozolino in his book "The
Neuroscience of Psychotherapy" one of the principles of
the brain is there is a great deal of back and forth
communication between the various parts –
from the top to the bottom and side to side*

*Another important principle is there is
a great deal of emphasis on balance*

*One part of the brain exists to inhibit another part
of the brain so that opposing brain functions
maintain a certain equilibrium*

*We also see this emphasis on balance
in the nervous system –
Cortical vs Sub-Cortical
And Sympathetic vs Parasympathetic
as well as in the chemical system –
Oxytocin vs Vasopressin*

*One function keeps the opposing function in check
which maintains homeostasis in the body*

*Our task then becomes determining
which part of the brain is the decision maker
And even more importantly
communicating with this decision maker
and influencing/regulating the decisions it is making*

*For instance suppose the Sympathetic Nervous System is
too activated and we end up feeling anxious all the time*

*Can we take some actions to calm the Sympathetic
Nervous System so that we are more peaceful*

*The answer is Yes
This can be done by approaching the problem
from several different directions*

George W. Barnard M.D.

According to Stephen Porges in his book "The Polyvagal Theory" one way is to activate the Parasympathetic Nervous System through the Modern Myelinated Vagus by altering our breathing pattern ("Myelinated" means that a Myelin sheath has formed around the nerve to allow the nerve impulses to move more quickly)

When we inhale we activate the Sympathetic Nervous System and when we exhale we activate the modern portion of the Parasympathetic Nervous System

So if we make the exhalation longer than the inhalation we put the Parasympathetic Nervous System in a more dominant position and we achieve a calming effect on the body

But how about handling some of the emotions – such as shame – in which we don't know which part of the brain is controlling the emotion/feeling

What do we do then

Here we use a different approach We know that we are not just one Self but instead are a multi-dimensional Self with different components

In the instance of shame – we can attribute experiencing that emotion to Judgmental Self that harshly judges and blames us as being flawed so that we feel very bad about ourselves and who we are

So what do we do to alleviate shame

*We call in an internal helper – an ally – our Divine Self
that unconditionally accepts us as we are*

*Divine Self is able to take away the negative feelings
associated with shame and replace them with the positive
emotions of love and acceptance so that
we regain our feelings of our self-worth*

This is a restorative process – a healing process

∞

George W. Barnard M.D.

One Integrated Brain

Just how many brains do we have anyway

*We hear talk of the old brain –
the new brain – and the limbic brain*

*We also hear about the right and left
hemispheres of the brain*

*But believe me there is only one
integrated brain with many components –
sometimes working in harmony –
sometimes working in opposition*

But there are certain principles that are operative

*Keep in mind that our present brain
did not just come about overnight*

*Rather our brain is an evolutionary brain that
came into existence over millions of years*

*The human brain has evolved based on the environmental
and internal challenges that our pre-human and human
ancestors encountered*

*Stephen Porges in his book "The Polyvagal Theory"
reports that our present human brain preserved some
features of the earlier models –
modified others – and developed new ones
not present in our ancient ancestors*

Unlocking Life's Secrets

*Some of the ancient inherited sub-cortical components
still operate today and influence/control
much of our behavior at a non-conscious level*

We are so proud of our newer cortical structures

*We like to think they make us so
different from other animals*

*This leads us to deny the power that the
older inherited brain structures have over us*

*This principle doesn't get discussed much –
it is like we try to keep relatives that we are
ashamed of hidden from view*

*However if we can accept the existence of both the cortical
(conscious) and the sub-cortical (non-conscious)
structures of our brains then we can more effectively deal
with them and even modify their functions*

*Over the course of time evolution has developed a
specialization of brain structures*

*While there is a great deal of communication between the
various components of the two brain hemispheres
(the right and left hemispheres) they do differ to some
degree as to what kind of behavior each hemisphere is
biased to dominate and control*

*For example Louis Cozolino in his book
"The Neuroscience of Psychotherapy" reports that the
right brain is biased toward the non-conscious –
non-verbal and emotional behavior whereas the
left hemisphere is biased toward the conscious –
verbal – problem solving behavior*

*Because of its strong connections with the older limbic
system and the viscera (the internal organs)
the right hemisphere has a strong influence on the
regulation of the Autonomic Nervous System
and the Endocrine System*

*This means that the right hemisphere is
more strongly activated during times of stress*

*The left hemisphere is more heavily associated with the
conscious mind whereas the right hemisphere
is associated with the unconscious mind*

*Usually we tend to think and act as though
we are consciously controlling all of our
thoughts – feelings – and behavior*

*But in reality the great majority of our brain activity is
taking place at a non-conscious level and therefore
outside of our conscious awareness*

*An example of this is when we meet a stranger and
immediately we feel safe and comfortable
with that individual*

*Then we give conscious explanations such as
"Oh he/she is such a friendly person"*

In reality all – or almost all – of the decision making about whether or not we are safe or in danger with a person is made by our ancient sub-cortical brain structures interpreting facial features – voice intonation – and body movement

All of this is implemented on a non-conscious level – with the right hemisphere more dominant during this appraisal process – preparing the body for responsive action if necessary

If danger is detected then we engage in defensive action – fight – flight – or freeze

If the environment is judged to be safe then we can approach the other for social interactions

In general the right hemisphere is biased toward the negative emotions and the left hemisphere is biased toward the positive emotions

Keep in mind that there is two-way communication between the two hemispheres as well as between the cortical and sub-cortical brain structures so that the brain functions as an integrated whole

For example the neuronal network linking the Orbital Medial Prefrontal Cortex with the Anterior Cingulate is necessary for us to experience empathy

If there is damage to either structure then our ability to empathize with the Other is limited

George W. Barnard M.D.

*Although it is an extremely complex structure –
in recent years research has shown that
we can communicate with the brain –
both verbally and non-verbally*

*For example on a non-verbal level we can
activate either the left or right hemisphere
by changing the directional gaze of our eyes*

*If we gaze our eyes to the right
we stimulate the left hemisphere and
thereby decrease our cortisol production
and other stress hormones*

*This same action also helps us to be
more optimistic and resilient*

*Another non-verbal technique of reducing
the influence of the right hemisphere of the brain
is to learn means of relaxation*

*This brings about a decrease in negative emotions
such as shame – guilt – and fear*

*With the use of verbal means of communication with the
brain such as imagination and visualization
we can also achieve desired
psychological and physiological states*

∞

Old and New Responses to Threat

We have several components to our nervous system:
The Central Nervous System
The Peripheral Nervous System and
The Autonomic Nervous System

There are two parts to the Autonomic Nervous System:
The Sympathetic Nervous System and
The Parasympathetic Nervous System

Much research has been done on the Sympathetic Nervous System but little attention has been given to the Parasympathetic Nervous System

One of the nerves in the brain – called the Vagus nerve – controls almost all of the Parasympathetic responses

Until recently it was believed that there was only one Vagus nerve but then Stephen Porges in his book "The Polyvagal Theory" discovered that in reality there are two components to the Vagus nerve – an ancient component (the "Unmyelinated" Vagus) and a modern component (the "Myelinated" Vagus)

Porges has described a sequential response of the three components of the Autonomic Nervous System to threat:

- The Modern Myelinated Vagus as the first response
- The Sympathetic Nervous System as the second response
- the Ancient Vagus as the third response to threat

George W. Barnard M.D.

First the Modern Myelinated Vagus helps to prevent a major outpouring of Adrenaline and Cortisol and acts as an inhibitory control of the Sympathetic Nervous System

If the Modern Myelinated Vagus does not control the threat then the Sympathetic Nervous System kicks in and becomes more dominant and prepares the body for mobilization and a stronger fight/flight response

*If this second response does not seem to control the threat and the person feels helpless and like death is imminent then the Ancient Unmyelinated Vagus is activated – initiating an immobilization/freeze response
At this time the person may feign fainting or death*

I observed a dramatic example of this sequential response in the early 1960s when we were conducting research in the Psychophysiological Stress Division of the Aerospace Medical Research Laboratories in Dayton, Ohio

In one of our projects we collected six different physiological measures from 88 male college students (or subjects) as they underwent five different stressors:
- *Having their blood drawn*
- *Watching a movie of traumatic war injuries*
- *Immersing a foot in a container of ice water*
- *Hearing their speech played back to them at a delayed interval*
- *Having their blood drawn a second time*

*For each stressor there was a separate period of
Rest – Anticipation – Stress – Recovery
10 (or 11%) of the 88 subjects experienced syncope (fainting) or indications of impending syncope*

*5 of the 10 subjects experienced fainting after the first
withdrawal of blood while the other five fainted
after viewing the traumatic war injuries or
having a foot immersed in ice water*

*This illustrates the brain falsely interpreting the event as
being more life-threatening than it was, and therefore the
Ancient Unmyelinated Vagus was activated*

*The emotional component of these stressors was
noteworthy. At times the physiological response to the
anticipated threat was as great as the actual stressor*

*Some subjects falsely evaluated the degree of threat on the
first withdrawal of blood with a drop in blood pressure
and heart rate which caused them to faint
These same subjects corrected this threat
evaluation on the second withdrawal of blood*

*Their blood pressure and heart rate did not fall below the
resting stage baseline and they did not faint
This illustrates that Stephen Porges' first two responders
– i.e. the Modern Myelinated Vagus and the Sympathetic
Nervous System – dealt with the perceived threat and it
was not necessary for the Ancient Unmyelinated Vagus
to be activated*

*These findings illustrate the sequencing of the three
components of the Autonomic Nervous System to stress
as described by Stephen Porges*

∞

George W. Barnard M.D.

Secrets of the Brain

*I bet you didn't know that our brains
are constantly making decisions for us
without our awareness or consent*

*According to Stephen Porges in his book
"The Polyvagal Theory" every time we meet a person
we see the individual with our eyes and this information
is passed to the temporal lobes of our brain*

*There the data is processed by the fusiform gyrus (FG)
and the superior temporal sulcus (STS)*

*They are the decision makers on
a very important issue in our lives
The FG and STS are sub-cortical brain structures
that decide whether the person is safe and trustworthy
or is a threat to us*

*The FG and STS make this decision
without consulting with us
The decision is made at a non-conscious level
of our being and has major consequences
on how we respond to the person*

*If the FG and STS decide the person is safe then we may
approach the individual for social engagement*

*But if the FG and STS decide the person is a threat then
our body prepares for one of three responses –
fight – flight – or freeze*

All this is done at a non-conscious level so that we are not aware of what is being decided or why

The FG and STS are making these critical decisions

They are generally depending almost entirely on non-verbal input such as the features of the face – the movements of the body – and the qualities of the voice

The decisions made by the FG and STS activate very complex neural circuits within the brain that prepare us for fight – flight – freeze responses whether we like it or not

The non-conscious decision making doesn't end there

Assume the FG and STS decide that the person we are observing is a threat – untrustworthy – even life-threatening

The FG and STS then send a message to the Amygdala located in the limbic system

The Amygdala communicates with the Periaqueductal Gray (PAG) – a mid-brain structure – and the PAG decides whether to confront – flee – or freeze

Either way the decision is made at a non-conscious level so that we are not aware of the process

We are only aware of our body responses to the decision Generally the non-conscious decisions made by the ancient components of our brain are correct

George W. Barnard M.D.

*But what about those times when the brain
makes the wrong appraisal
What if the brain falsely assesses the person
to be a threat when she/he is actually safe*

*In this instance the brain will be send out command
signals for the body – especially the Sympathetic Nervous
System to produce stress chemicals such as Cortisol and
Adrenaline that – in reality – are not needed*

*These chemicals which increase our heart rate – blood
pressure – and other physiological functions often
negatively affect our thinking – emotions and behavior*

*These chemicals prepare us for a battle that –
in reality – we do not need to engage in*

*They also affect our desire and ability
to interact with others because
they distort our perception of others*

Is there a way out of this puzzle

*Well it just may be that becoming aware
of this situation helps us*

*We can begin to pay close attention to our body and
develop a sensitivity to how it responds to different cues
from the environment and from our mind*

*We can make these observations more objectively in our
role as Observer-Witness Self than we can as Ego*

*With practice we can notice the relationship between our
body reactions and the environment
(both external and internal)*

*Then we can apply our knowledge of self-regulation to
bring the Sympathetic Nervous System under some
degree of control before it becomes too activated*

∞

George W. Barnard M.D.

Evolutionary Brain

*Our brain is not just our brain
It is also the brain of our human and pre-human
ancestors going back millions of years
Some scientists have said that in fact
we have three brains in one*

*Evolution has a way of keeping
parts of ancient systems that have worked well –
discarding those components that have not worked well –
and modifying/creating systems to serve new functions*

*So you might say that while our ancient
ancestors have evolved from the amphibians and reptiles
we still carry bits and pieces of them with us*

*In the evolutionary process when
animals came out of the water and onto land
they faced different challenges
and thus different body systems were needed*

*For example with the transition from
reptiles to mammals there was a major shift from
the hatching of eggs to live births*

*Major changes – including the development of
the brain and nervous system – occurred with humans*

*One critical development was that the volume of the
cortex portion of the brain greatly increased –
permitting more complex functions to be available*

Unlocking Life's Secrets

*Up until the development of mammals
evolution had focused heavily on neural changes
whose aim was detecting danger/threat
and providing hormonal and motor systems
that supported fight-flight-freeze behaviors*

*But with mammals – especially humans –
evolution developed brain and other physical changes
that not only carried out the assessment of threat
but also helped to cope with the threat*

*In addition evolution also developed neural/chemical
systems that – in the absence of threat –
could initiate/enhance social behaviors*

*These social behaviors were necessary to support
prolonged periods of dependency in infancy/childhood –
a unique quality of mammals – especially humans*

*Let's look in detail at some of these changes
as reported by Kerstin Moberg and Roberta Francis
in their book "The Oxytocin Factor"*

*One of the most important changes was the
emergence of the hormone Oxytocin that facilitates
the bonding between mother and infant*

*Oxytocin also performs a number of vital functions
in the body – including the integration of
emotional and social functions*

But perhaps one of the most important functions of Oxytocin is to inhibit the activity of the Amygdala – an important part of the limbic system that helps us deal with danger or the threat of danger

This inhibition has a major calming effect and therefore some have called Oxytocin the anti-stress hormone

Stephen Porges in his book "The Polyvagal Theory" reports on three other very important developments that occurred in our evolutionary process

First: While reptiles only have an Ancient Unmyelinated Vagus – in mammals the Vagal neural pathways became more complex with the development of an additional component – the Modern Myelinated Vagus

Second: A three-tiered hierarchical and sequential response to threat/danger developed in humans

Third: In the absence of danger – through the development of the Modern Myelinated Vagus (along with Oxytocin) – humans developed a very complex social system which facilitated the growth of the family and community unit

Keep in mind that until the emergence of humans the evolutionary trend had been to support animals in the presence of a danger or a threat to either stay and fight – flee – or feign death

*The feigning of death was made possible by
the Ancient Unmyelinated Vagus*

*The stay and fight and the flee responses
were made possible by the development of the
Sympathetic Nervous System*

*With the development of the Modern Myelinated Vagus
in humans a new tool was brought into play*

*Porges explains that the Modern Myelinated Vagus
is an element of the three-tiered hierarchical and
sequential response to threat that
evolution developed in humans*

*He states that in the first level of dealing with a threat
humans have the capability of using the Modern
Myelinated Vagus to prevent a major outpouring of the
stress hormones Cortisol and Adrenaline*

*If this first level does not contain the threat then the
Sympathetic Nervous System is activated with
an outpouring of stress hormones*

*If this level does not contain the threat then the
Ancient Unmyelinated Vagus is activated
with the feigning of death*

*Clearly the evolutionary process as discussed by both
Porges and Moberg has helped us develop tools to deal
with threats and stress more effectively*

While Oxytocin is a chemical system that existed millions of years before the neural Modern Myelinated Vagus existed – both joined together to create significant preventive and protective anti- stress properties

The part of the Body/Brain that makes the decision concerning when Oxytocin and the Modern Myelinated Vagus will produce these anti-stress properties takes place without our awareness

In the past this decision-making process was considered automatic and not under our conscious control

However more recently scientists have found that we can communicate with these functions and influence their effect on us

When we are able to influence these functions we take a significant step in preventing/countering the destructive results of chronic stress

∞

Humans Become Social Beings

*Assume for a moment that you were present at the time
when evolution made the transition
from pre-human primates to humans*

*Assume further that you were a design engineer
for the human species
and were asked to help design humans*

Here is your task

*Up to this moment evolution had focused on our
pre-human ancestors detecting danger and
protecting themselves from harm
by mobilizing the body to either
fight or flee the scene of danger*

*This mobilization strategy was made possible
by the Sympathetic branch of the
Autonomic Nervous System*

*In addition to the mobilization strategy there was also a
more ancient immobilization defense system
in which the animal feigned death*

*This strategy was carried out by lowering the metabolism
of the body and activating the
Ancient Unmyelinated Vagus – a component
of the Parasympathetic branch of the
Autonomic Nervous System*

*Now here is where you and
your design skills come into play*

George W. Barnard M.D.

As part of the evolution team you are asked to create a proposal to link the Autonomic Nervous System to social behaviors among those in close proximity

You can do this by either modifying existing neural systems or developing new ones

So what is your plan

Well we will never know what you decided to do

What we do know – according to Stephen Porges as discussed in his book "The Polyvagal Theory" – is what actually developed through the course of evolution

First: The two older strategies for coping with danger – i.e. mobilization (via the Sympathetic Nervous System) and immobilization (via the Ancient Unmyelinated Vagus) – were left intact

Second: New neural components of the Autonomic Nervous System were brought into existence to create a third subsystem (via the Modern Myelinated Vagus) that not only adds more flexibility to deal with danger but also greatly facilitates pro-social behaviors in humans

Third: All three subsystems (i.e. the Ancient Unmyelinated Vagus – the Sympathetic Nervous System – and the Modern Myelinated Vagus) were hierarchically linked together so that in the presence of danger they are called into action sequentially:

- *First the newest subsystem (i.e. the Modern Myelinated Vagus) is called into action to manage the danger*

- *If that strategy is ineffective then the Sympathetic Nervous System – with its mobilization strategy – is called upon next*
- *If that strategy is also ineffective the final recourse is the Ancient Unmyelinated Vagus with its immobilization strategy*

Fourth: The third subsystem of the Autonomic Nervous System (i.e. the Modern Myelinated Vagus – which some refer to as the "social brain") provides behavioral strategies for humans in a safe environment to:

- *Form close and intimate relationships*
- *Communicate with one another from infancy through old age*
- *carry out self-regulatory functions of body and behavior that are extremely important when humans are responding to stress*

How is all of this accomplished – you may ask

The answer – according to Porges – is "the emergence of the brain - face - heart circuit"

"Wow" – you reply – "tell me more about this magical circuit"

This circuit came into existence through the course of evolution

Essentially this brain - face - heart circuit is composed of cranial nerves V, VII, IX, X and XI and brings into existence functions that did not exist previously

Cranial Nerve X – which is referred to as the Vagus nerve (the main Parasympathetic component of the Autonomic Nervous System) – has two main branches:

1. *An ancient branch that is unmyelinated and is known as the Vegetative Vagus or the Ancient Unmyelinated Vagus*

   This branch primarily influences the internal organs below the diaphragm and is in control of the freeze/feign death reaction of the Autonomic Nervous System

2. *A modern branch that is myelinated and is known as the Smart Vagus or the Modern Myelinated Vagus*

   This branch primarily influences internal organs above the diaphragm – particularly the heart and lungs

   It serves as a "vagal brake" to modulate and dampen Sympathetic output so that the body can engage in challenges without a massive outpouring of the stress hormones Adrenaline and Cortisol

In addition the Smart Vagus is connected with cranial nerves V, VII, IX, and XI – permitting them to be intimately involved with our emotions and social communications network

*These four cranial nerves carry out functions that are
influenced/controlled both by
cortical (conscious/voluntary) and
sub-cortical (non-conscious/involuntary)
components of our brain*

*This means that these four cranial nerves influence
behavioral responses not only that
we consciously and intentionally want to occur but also
those that we display to others
without our awareness or intent*

*For example cranial nerve VII controls
the muscles of our facial expression and
reflect the emotions of our internal feeling state of being
These facial expressions have great significance in
communicating to others what we are feeling and whether
or not we pose a threat to them*

*Another example is cranial nerve IX
This nerve controls the muscles used for
swallowing and for vocalization
They also reflect our internal emotional state and
carry a message to others if we are trustworthy
or if we pose a danger to others*

*A final example is cranial nerve XI
This nerve controls the muscles of the neck and thereby
head-turning/tilting that also reflect our internal
emotional state and attitude to the other*

*All of these examples illustrate that the striated muscles
of our face – head/neck – and throat – all under both
voluntary and involuntary control – as well as the
smooth muscles of our heart and bronchi – usually under
involuntary control – make mammals –
and especially humans – unique*

*These complex neuronal structures – along with
Oxytocin – enhance our abilities as social beings –
in a safe environment – to live together as a
community and support one another
with love and compassion*

*These are traits that not only will
aid in the survival of the species but will also
bring happiness to ourselves and to others*

We have a choice:

*To live and function in a state that
reflects an Ego-dominance
which is primarily concerned about
our own selfish needs or
to live and function in a state that reflects
Divine Self-dominance
which is concerned not only about our own needs
but also about the needs of others*

*It all begins with our intent
Then we need to become aware of
how we are interacting with others
And finally we need to be willing to treat others
as we desire to be treated*

∞

How Our BodyMindSpirit Communicates

Candace Pert in her book "Everything You Need to Know to Feel Go(o)d" reports that in the 17th Century an agreement was reached between the Pope and a philosopher named Descartes that still has repercussions on the way the medical profession today views the connection of the body with the mind

*When Descartes sought permission from the Pope to study human corpses he agreed to study only the body and leave the study of the soul to the church
This agreement artificially separated the human into body and mind and has hindered Western medicine from viewing the person as a unified entity*

*Regretfully some of this false belief in the importance of separating the mind and body exists even today
It has fostered the materialistic belief that only the body is real and that the mind and soul are not real*

In recent years however there has been strong evidence to show that we are a single unit

We are BodyMindSpirit

Indeed we are both material and non-material

While we have different systems in the body such as the Nervous – Cardiovascular – Digestive – Reproductive – Immune – and Respiratory systems – they are all united

*There is not only communication across physical systems
but also between material and non-material components*

*What exists at one moment in a physical form
may be transformed in the next moment into a
psychic/emotional/mental/spiritual reality*

*And this transformation from one form of reality
into another goes both ways –
from material to non-material and
from non-material to material*

*Just as light can exist as either a wave or a particle
so too can our BodyMindSpirit unit
exist one moment as a polypeptide
(e.g. endorphin – a material reality)
and the next instant as an emotion
(e.g. euphoria – a non-material or emotional reality)*

*Take note of the prior sentence because
it should be an "Aha" moment for you*

*This complex – flexible – integrated system is called a
Psychosomatic Communications Network (PSCN)*

How does this ancient but very efficient system work

*Candace Pert in her book "Molecules of Emotions"
states that it all begins with a single molecule –
called an information substance receptor*

*This molecule is located on the surface of cells in the
body/brain and functions as a sensor
The information substance receptor waits to
pick up messages from another information
substance – called a ligand*

*These ligands travel throughout the body
in the extra-cellular fluid*

*The ligand–receptor cell dyads
(also referred to as the chemical brain)
form a powerful communications unit
that existed long before the brain-nervous
system component (also referred to
as the electrical brain) came into existence*

*The chemical system exists throughout the body/brain
and when activated remains a powerful force for longer
periods of time than does the electrical system*

*The chemical system produces our moods
which can last for prolonged periods*

*As part of the chemical system both the receptors and the
ligands are vibrating separately throughout the body*

*When the receptor receives a specific resonance
from a ligand they bind together
An informational message is then received into the cell
and the cell performs the required action*

When enough of these receptor – ligand units are working together these material substances are transformed into non-material phenomena such as emotions and moods or different states of awareness The receptors are very specific and respond only to ligands that meet their defined specifications

The ligands consist of three chemical types: neurotransmitters – steroids – peptides The peptides play the major role in the transfer of information throughout the body and from one system (such as the nervous system) to another system (such as the immune system)

Pert has reported that scientists have estimated that these ligands transport 98% of all data transferred in our body/brain unit – with the other 2% taking place at the neuronal synapse

Candace Pert's theory – as she explains in her book "Molecules of Emotions" – is that the neuropeptides (a string of amino acids) are the molecular material substrate for the non-material experiences that we have – such as thoughts – sensations – feelings – emotions – drives – even states of awareness

She refers to the ligands with their receptors as "the molecules of emotion"

The neuropeptides as neurotransmitters travel great distances throughout the body and brain carrying their informational messages regarding what to do and when to do it

*These messages are not only carried to different parts of
the body but they are also stored throughout the body
(not just the brain) as memories*

*And look at this flexibility – a ligand polypeptide
functioning in one part of the body can bring about
one body action whereas the same ligand functioning
in another part of the body brings about
an entirely different body action*

*Keep in mind that almost all of this transfer of
information is done at a non-conscious level
so that we are not aware of the process*

*Remember that all of our different systems
such as the nervous – cardiovascular – and immune
systems are linked together*

*There is constant communication between different
systems and yet there is only
one unified BodyMindSpirit Unit*

*We can access this Psychosomatic Communication
Network and experience healing transformation
We can access this Network through various means –
such as meditation - visualization –
bodywork – music – and breath control*

*Through the use of these methods we can also experience
for ourselves the great value of not only coming into
contact with deeper states of being within ourselves
but also experiencing the presence and
transformative/healing powers of the Divine Spirit*

George W. Barnard M.D.

I first came into contact with the Psychosomatic Communications Network in a major way when I was at the Aerospace Medical Research Laboratories - Wright Patterson Air Force Base in Dayton Ohio

My psychiatric residency was sponsored by the Air Force Following my residency I was assigned to the Stress and Fatigue Section (later renamed the Psychophysiological Stress Division)

Our mission was to anticipate some of the body-mind stresses that the astronauts would encounter in space – determine their effect – and then see what we might do to counter their negative effects and enhance the positive body-mind functions

We could not duplicate the zero gravity effects of space but we could approximate some of effects by submerging the subjects in a tank of water

Previous studies had shown that immersion of the body (except for the head) in water produces a significant increase in diuresis (increase in urine flow) in humans in one hour

In one of our studies we wanted to see if self-hypnosis and the suggestion of thirst could alter the body-mind functions and inhibit this diuresis The results of the experiment were very clear and published in the Psychosomatic Medicine by Michael McCalley and me

*We found that indeed diuresis could be inhibited by
means of self-hypnosis and the suggestion of thirst*

*We postulated that this inhibition came about as result of
the self-hypnosis plus the suggestion of thirst that
triggered a release of the Anti-Diuretic Hormone causing
an increased reabsorption of urine by the kidneys*

*And guess what – the Anti-Diuretic Hormone is also
known as Vasopressin – a polypeptide that is an
Informational Substance or ligand and is part of the
Psychosomatic Communications Network
that we have been discussing*

*To me this is an example of the power of the
BodyMindSpirit complex to communicate with
components within this complex and to carry out a form
of self-regulation altering the way the body functions*

*Indeed I believe that it illustrates the
ongoing transformation between the non-material
form of reality and the material form of reality*

*For example self-hypnosis and the suggestion of thirst –
which are both forms of a non-material
state of reality – increased the formation of the
Information Substance – Vasopressin –
a material reality – which inhibited the diuresis*

*This understanding creates great optimism for our
future knowledge of how the BodyMindSpirit functions
and how we might best alter it in order to improve
our physical – mental – spiritual health*

∞

George W. Barnard M.D.

Perils of the Danger-O-Stat

*You may have heard of therm-o-stats
but I bet that you have never heard of Danger-O-Stats*

*Therm-o-stats kick in when a certain temperature is
reached and activate a furnace/air conditioner
to raise or lower the ambient temperature*

*Danger-O-Stats kick in when a certain level
of danger is detected and activate our bodies
to prepare to fight – flee – or freeze (i.e. immobilize)*

*We all have Danger-O-Stats – we just don't know it
They are part of our evolutionary heritage
originating millions of years ago*

*They are built into the Sub-Cortical part of our brains
and operate almost exclusively on a non-conscious basis
so that – for the most part – we are not aware of them*

*These neuronal systems receive information from the
external environment as well as from the internal
environment of our bodies and our brains*

*This means that our eyes may bring a stimulus
indicating danger or our minds also may bring a
thought/memory indicating danger*

*But both can activate the Danger-O-Stat whether the
danger is truly present and accurately interpreted
or is imagined or falsely interpreted*

Unlocking Life's Secrets

*For example suppose two teenage boys meet
and one of them says something derogatory
about the other boy's mother*

*These inflammatory words realistically are not dangerous
to the offended boy but
they trigger his internal Danger-O-Stat*

*The Sympathetic Nervous System of the offended boy
hearing these words is activated – he goes into a rage –
pulls out a gun and shoots and kills the offender*

All in a matter of seconds

*This is a rather dramatic example of an evolutionary
component of our bodies designed to help our survival but
instead has gone astray and backfired*

*Almost daily many of us experience minor –
sometimes major – interactions that trigger a
toned-down but similar stressful experience*

*According to Sonia Lupien in her book "Well Stressed",
the four experiences that will trigger a stress reaction are:*

*Novelty
Uncertainty
Threat to Ego
Sense that we are losing control*

(Acronym – NUTS)

George W. Barnard M.D.

We run into situations in which our Egos are threatened but our brains/minds/bodies react as though we have encountered a severe danger – such as we are being attacked by a tiger threatening our very existence

According to scientific literature these non-conscious neural systems – that I am calling Danger-O-Stats – are accurate in some people but not in others – and that is where the problems begin

It seems that some individuals live as though they are in a constant state of danger

Threatening events trigger an activation of the Sympathetic Nervous System with an outpouring of the stress hormones – Adrenaline and Cortisol

Stephen Porges in his book "The Polyvagal Theory" reports that there is an evolutionary principle that has three tiers of response to stress – with the most recent tier responding first

On the first tier the Modern Myelinated Vagus kicks in to prevent an outpouring of Adrenaline and Cortisol

If that is not sufficient to control the threat the second tier is activated with an activation of the Sympathetic Nervous System – causing an increased heart rate and blood pressure

*If this is not sufficient to contain the threat and
the organism senses an imminent threat of death
the third tier is activated by a massive Ancient
Unmyelinated Vagus response*

*This response can include physiological drops in blood
pressure and heart rate which result
in fainting or feigning death*

*Well – suppose that we are part of this group
that is hyper-alert to the perception of danger –
real or imagined – what are we to do*

*The first step is to admit that we are part of this group
and take ownership of this complex pattern of behavior*

*Then we need to decide if we want to change the pattern
or keep repeating a destructive repetitive cycle of
behavior that frequently leads to interpersonal conflicts*

*If we do want to change and let go of this
behavioral complex – how do we do it*

*It all goes back to integration – coordination – and
balance of complex neural structures*

*We begin by changing the dominance control links
between our conscious Cortical brain (the Orbital Medial
Prefrontal Cortex) and our non-conscious
Sub-Cortical brain (the Amygdala)*

George W. Barnard M.D.

*According to Louis Cozolino in his book
"The Neuroscience of Psychotherapy" it is the
Orbital Medial Prefrontal Cortex that can provide the
inhibitory actions necessary to control the Amygdala
and prevent an unwarranted activation
of the Sympathetic Nervous System*

*This can be done by learning breathing techniques
that strengthen the Modern Myelinated Vagus
and relaxation techniques that
change the dominance balance between
the Orbital Medial Prefrontal Cortex and the Amygdala*

*Naturally all this will require
knowledge – practice – and patience*

∞

Getting in Harmony with the Eternal

It's my choice – my decision alone

*I can choose to exist only in the material world
If so – I remain feeling charged up –
stressed out – full of fear*

*But I can also choose to open myself to the spiritual
reality wherein I have access to the Infinite
I can encounter the Divine and bring myself
in harmony with the inflow of the Eternal*

*This Energy – this Wisdom – flowing throughout
my body and brain is mine to be tapped –
bringing me almost unlimited fulfillment*

*I can reach the state of ruah – that place of inner
calm that exists even in the moments
of life's greatest turbulence*

*For instance – suppose a person is extremely angry at me
and says something very degrading to me
This is a threat to Ego and in a split second
the Amygdala of my old brain detects danger and
becomes activated preparing me for fight or flight*

*The Amygdala immediately fires up the
Hypothalamic-Pituitary-Adrenal Axis (HPAA)
and the Stress chemicals flow –
giving me the necessary energy to do battle*

*Here comes the front line troops –
Cortisol and Adrenaline*

George W. Barnard M.D.

But wait a minute

*I can also take action to call in my helpers
I pause briefly and focus on my breathing –
prolonging the exhalation phase
so it is longer than the inhalation phase –
thus activating my Modern Myelinated Vagus*

*I turn inward and enter my Meditative State
I use my imagination and visualization to activate my
Prefrontal Cortex as well as call on the Hypothalamus to
release Oxytocin – my anti-stress hormone
All of these measures are aimed to find calming factors
to counter the effects of Cortisol and Adrenaline*

*The modern brain communicates with the ancient brain
and the conscious communicates with the unconscious*

The rational reassures and calms the irrational

*Now Observer-Witness Self rather than Ego
can make a decision regarding which
action – if any – I should take*

*Observer-Witness Self can decide for me
not to do battle with the offender and not to run
but to stay and listen – shema
To stay and negotiate – even to stay and show
compassion and understanding – even forgiveness*

And guess what – it all begins with my intention

∞

Experiencing the Power of the Amygdala

*It started out as a rather bland statement
but when I received it – in a very brief time –
it had become much more*

*Somehow my internal monitors had picked up a
danger signal and it was spreading through my body*

*At first it was just vague internal body feelings
that I had difficulty identifying
But then as I carefully observed them
they were much more*

*What started out as just visceral rumblings
were rapidly developing into a churning volcano*

*I knew that I could not process this complex mess as Ego
so I called on Observer-Witness Self for help*

*Then I took several deep breaths
and entered a Meditative State*

*Since I had no conscious memory of where
these feelings were coming from
I asked my imaginative mind to
take me back in time to an occasion
that took place containing similar feelings*

*And there I was – 10 years old –
back in my small hometown*

George W. Barnard M.D.

*I was at a neighbor's house visiting
a friend and his family*

Suddenly everyone had left the room and I was alone

*That's strange I thought
Something funny is going on
I will hide in the room and see what happens*

*After a while someone entered the room and said
"He's gone now – ya'll can come back in" –
and they did*

*"Now that he's gone we can have our dessert"
the mother said*

*As I watched I had the definite feeling that
I was not welcome*

*I was bombarded with a mixture of feelings
Sadness – Anger – Shame – Confusion – Embarrassment*

*But most of all –
Rejection –
painful rejection*

And I didn't know what to do

*So without saying a word
I walked out of the room*

*And then my tears began to flow –
and flow they did for some time*

Unlocking Life's Secrets

But flowing tears did not solve my problem –
I was still stuck with the puzzle

Why was I being rejected in this manner

Had I overstayed my welcome on other occasions

Had I been there at meal times and
eaten food that was scarce
or was I just an obnoxious kid
that they didn't want around

To this day I still don't have any answers

But I do know this

There have been other occasions throughout the years
when I have sensed rejection – rightly or wrongly

And again my Amygdala has flooded me
with a mixture of powerful emotions

Over time I have tried different ways
of dealing with these painful feelings

What I have definitely learned is
I had better not deny them

For me what has worked best is to
take ownership of them

These feelings are mine –
but they are not me –
I am more

*I have learned that once I admit ownership
I do not have to act out in a
destructive way to deal with them*

*Sometimes simply labeling the emotion
I am feeling is enough to decrease the
arousal response of the Amygdala –
but it usually takes more*

*I have found it best not to deal with them
while I am functioning as Ego
Instead I call on higher states of the Total Self –
i.e. Observer-Witness Self and Divine Self –
to carry out the negotiations with Judgmental Self*

*Judgmental Self will berate me and attempt to
make me feel bad about myself by pouring on the
negative feelings of guilt and shame*

*Observer-Witness Self – with the help of the
Orbital Medial Prefrontal Cortex –
can obtain some objectivity and a
higher level of integration and self-regulation*

*Divine Self can remove some of the feelings of
self-blame and agitation and help me attain
more self-compassion and self-acceptance –
even for attributes that I would prefer not to have*

*Throughout the years I have learned that
my Danger-O-Stat is set too low for situations
involving potential abandonment or rejection*

*On those occasions I must caution myself
about the actual degree of danger present
because these trigger-point stimuli stored away
in my implicit memories will activate my Amygdala*

*I have come to respect the power of the Amygdala
but not to feel helpless when it is called into action*

*I know that I have internal allies who are
just as powerful and can assist me in this process*

*To me it's all about learning about
my process of self-regulation*

*This is a process that begins in infancy –
if not in the womb –
and continues throughout life*

*We are just beginning to learn ways of
communicating with our different states of being –
many of which function on a
non-conscious plane of awareness*

*We can learn how to access them better
and have a two-way interchange with them*

*Learning how to communicate with these forces
will enable us to open our minds and hearts
so that we can allow love and other powerful healing
energies to flow freely throughout our being*

∞

George W. Barnard M.D.

The Wonders of Oxytocin

*It was about 1:30 A.M.
when she turned over in bed and said
"Honey – I keep rolling and tossing
but I can't get to sleep"*

*He had been here before and knew what to do –
"Turn over and lay on your back" he said
and she did*

*There was little need to talk
That would only waken her more*

*No – what was needed in this moment was for him
to communicate with our ally –
the Modern Myelinated Vagus*

*It would be the messenger carrier
and his fingers would send the message*

*Very lightly – very gently –
he began to stroke her belly
in a circular fashion
at about 40 strokes per minute
In less than five minutes he could hear her
breathing patterns change and then a light snore*

*He knew that she was asleep but he continued
the light touch pattern for several more minutes
to make sure she was sound asleep*

*When she awoke the next morning
she greeted him with a smile and said
"Thank you – the magic worked again"*

*"It was no magic" he replied
"It was the power of Oxytocin"*

*"Hey" – you may say
"That Oxytocin is powerful –
where can I get some of that"*

*You might be surprised to learn that
we already have it
It is available for all of us*

*Oxytocin is our anti-stress hormone that works
on many parts of our body as a "calming agent"*

*It helps to take away our fears and
soothes our BodyMindSpirit*

It is also the elixir that connects us with others

Let's trace the whole process

*The skin on the front of our body has special thin
slow-conducting nerve fibers that carry signals of
light touch directly to the more ancient parts of the brain
through the Modern Myelinated Vagus nerve*

*These signals are sent without entering the spinal cord –
which thick fast-conducting nerve fibers on other parts of
the body are required to do for normal touch*

George W. Barnard M.D.

*The Modern Myelinated Vagus transports the light
touch signals directly to the Hypothalamus*

*As the decision maker the Hypothalamus instructs the
Pituitary to release the Oxytocin into other parts of the
brain and the body to calm not only
the physiological systems of the body but also
the emotional systems of the mind*

*These neural/chemical substrates of the emotional
systems that make up our Calm – Connecting System
facilitate our ability to trust others and
develop relationships with them*

*Since so many folk are stressed out these days
it may be an ideal time for all of us to learn
how we can communicate with our body
to bring about the production and release of this
wonderful anti-stress hormone*

∞

Unlocking One of Life's Secrets

*There Bill was –
a 91 year old veteran
standing on the beaches of Normandy
71 years after he was first there on June 6 1944*

The beaches look quite different now than they did then

*The first time he was on this beach
he was standing on the bow of his ship
when it hit an explosive mine in the water
and his ship was blown up
He was injured in the explosion
but was one of the lucky ones that survived*

*His first memory after being rescued from the water
was seeing a red haired nurse standing before him*

*He was agitated – frightened – disoriented
But it took only one touch of the nurse
gently brushing his hair
to calm and soothe him*

*He took a deep breath – relaxed –
and fell into a deep peaceful sleep*

*71 years later he said the touch from his nurse
was just like the ones
he had received from his mother
when he was a small child*

George W. Barnard M.D.

*That touch had been just as powerful
when he was 19
as it was when he was 4
as it is now at age 91*

*What is going on here
How can a touch be so powerful
How can a touch have so much meaning*

*As Candace Pert discusses in her book
"Everything You Need to Know About Go(o)d"
the simple answer is that our BodyBrain is part of our
Psychosomatic Communication Network –
a communication network that unites us*

*We are not body and mind and spirit
We are BodyMindSpirit
A term that reflects our wholeness
A term that reflects our oneness*

*The Psychosomatic Communication Network
allows us to bridge the gap
so that we can go from one state of reality to another
We can go from existing as matter
to existing as non-matter*

*For example – when the mother or nurse touched Bill
she activated the release of Oxytocin –
an anti-stress hormone (a matter state) that triggered
a feeling state of calmness – peacefulness – bonding
(a non-matter state)*

*This Psychosomatic Communication Network
goes both ways – from matter to non-matter
or from non-matter to matter*

*We can experience a Meditative State (a non-matter
state) which can transform or modify how our body is
functioning (a matter state)*

*An example of this is Jen – a 40 year old woman who
experienced so much pain and discomfort from shingles
that she could not tolerate clothes touching her skin*

*She was able to become pain-free after learning how to
enter a Meditative State using imagination and
visualization to recall how she felt and functioned
prior to the onset of shingles*

*Essentially she was rerouting a path of information to the
brain used in the past when she was functioning
normally and thereby bypassing the dysfunctional
paths that exist in the present due to her shingles*

*Once the dynamics and mechanisms of the
Psychosomatic Communication Network
are understood and applied
we have unlocked one of life's
most important principles
and can use this understanding
to support the healing process*

O what joy!!

∞

George W. Barnard M.D.

Learning Self-Regulation

*Did you ever wonder how we learn to
regulate our internal processes –
especially how we learn to regulate our feelings*

We certainly can't do it when we are first born

*At that time we are almost entirely dependent on our
primary caretaker – usually our mother*

*Well – research is beginning to
shed light on this question*

*When we are with our mother as an infant
she carries out functions that influence or control
our internal body – brain behavior*

*At this time we begin to form an internal representation
of this person within our brain – as a form of imprinting*

*These representations are stored as implicit memory
in the Orbital Medial Prefrontal Cortex
and Sub-Cortical systems*

*We modify these early representations as we develop
In fact because of the plasticity of the brain –
we modify this virtual reality throughout life*

*Later – during times of stress – we automatically access
these internal caregivers and use them to either
bring ourselves comfort or distress*

*All of this occurs at a non-conscious level of awareness
so we have little or no idea of
what decisions our brain has made*

*Our brain makes these decisions from its assessment –
Is this a safe environment
If so I can stay*

*Is this environment a danger
If so then I must either prepare for battle or flee*

*Just stop and think for a minute what repercussions
this can have on a relationship or a marriage*

*Imagine a husband is in a conversation with his wife
Without the husband's conscious awareness
the pitch of the wife's voice becomes higher
or the muscles of her face tighten*

*Bingo – the husband's Amygdala has just been activated
because his non-conscious sensors in the sub-cortical
brain system have assessed danger to be present
and now prepares him for action*

*But here is where his early relationship
with his primary caregiver comes into play*

*If his caregiver had been attuned to
his signs of distress when he was an infant
then the caregiver had taken measures
to relieve him by regulating and soothing
the Autonomic Nervous System*

*The caregiver did this through gentle stroking –
a soft voice – eye contact – and a smiling face –
to reassure him that he was in a safe environment
with a person that he could trust*

*All of these actions taken by his caregiver
restored his internal balance
(again this occurs at a non-conscious level)*

*This early shaping of his body's
equilibrium has shown him the way*

*Now as an adult he can use meditation –
imagination – visualization – and breathing
techniques to bring about his own
self-regulatory homeostatic balance*

*But how about if his caretaker did not
provide the calming and comforting behaviors
which restored his internal balance – then what*

Well – we can take hope

*Even as an adult the plasticity of our brain permits us
to learn these self-calming behaviors*

*By using our ability to enter a Meditative State
and then using our imagination
we can create a special caregiver that is
available – capable – and willing
to bring about the much needed self-calming state*

*And the beauty is that
our brain responds as though it is real*

*Because it is real –
peace and harmony are restored
to our body and our mind*

*Once we have learned to do this
we practice – practice – practice*

We'll be glad we did

∞

George W. Barnard M.D.

Bonding Behavior

She had just become a grandmother for the first time

*Now she was on the floor
with her two month old grandson*

It was my pleasure to watch them lovingly interact

*In some ways it was like watching
two violinists giving a concert on stage*

Except now it was all nonverbal behavior

*Their eyes locked onto each other's faces
giving off those powerful signals of communication*

*She – with a quiet calm voice
speaking words of reassurance
He – with his smiles and cooing sounds
signaling his pleasure*

*Each seemed to know how to play her/his role –
both of giving and receiving
the powerful nonverbal messages*

*The result was a wonderful
synchrony between them*

*The mystery to me as the observer
was how in the world is this possible*

*Neither of them had been taught
how to play his/her individual role*

*There were no books on how to
perform this marvelous dance*

*It was the right hemisphere of one brain
talking to the right hemisphere of the other brain*

One age 57 years – the other age 2 months

*At times there were signs of minor disruption
in the homeostasis of the infant
The grandmother received the nonverbal
message of distress – assessed the problem – and
quickly implemented a solution to resolve the issue –
whether it was nursing him with a bottle of milk –
changing a soiled diaper or simply stroking his belly
to help him relax and become calm*

*Now certainly the grandmother had no conscious
knowledge that this rhythmic stroking of his belly
produces a release of the hormone Oxytocin that enhances
the calming/bonding process*

And yet there she was performing this action like a pro

*It was like the two parties had built-in
decision makers that permitted them to elicit
just the right response at just the right time*

Certainly a beautiful human interaction to witness

*And yet this is just the process that we all
go through when we are infants*

George W. Barnard M.D.

*At that time we are totally dependent
on our primary caretakers to take care of
our basic needs if we are to survive*

*Since we are unable at this young age
to regulate our own body system needs
we must be with someone who will assist us*

*It is through their help that we learn
to self-regulate our systems and responses to others*

*It is at this time that we learn or fail to learn
the self-calming and self-comforting behaviors needed
during and after times of stress*

*Learning these essential behaviors will enhance
our coping skills throughout our lifetime*

∞

Chapter 6: Stress

The Overstressed Mom

*As the mother of two children with asthma
she lived in constant dread*

*At night she tried to sleep
but always with one ear awake
to listen for the wheeze - the cough
that indicated a full blown attack was imminent*

*She remembers with horror
that night of terror*

*Her son couldn't get enough air
no matter how hard he tried*

*He came into her room with panic in his eyes
as he gasped desperately for air*

*Struggling in vain to get oxygen
he turned blue and almost passed out*

She feared certain loss

*A quick prayer emerged from her lips
Please God - not now -
have mercy*

*The 911 call -
the wait for the ambulance to arrive*

George W. Barnard M.D.

*It was not reassuring to see the look of desperation
on the faces of the paramedics
as they sought to revive her helpless child*

*The ride to the hospital seemed to take forever –
followed by the frantic activity
in the emergency room*

*After the acute crisis ended
she struggled with the trench wars
brought on by the negative effects
of the asthma medication –
headaches – hyperactivity – irritability –
altered sleeping patterns – emotional roller coaster –
feelings easily hurt – nothing pleased him*

*Children – usually delightful
while not on this activating medication –
suddenly and painfully turned into miserable beings
who insisted she share their misery*

*All these scenes – and more –
passed through her mind again and again –
often triggered by a single cough in the night*

*And then the recurring thoughts:
"What kind of mother am I"
"Have I done all I should do"*

*Although both children
were under the care of their doctors
these self-doubts still lingered*

Unlocking Life's Secrets

*These self-doubts indicated once again the heavy hand of
the Judgmental Self – that internal critic who never
seems to sleep and insists on having company –
causing her to experience self-blame and self-accusation*

*Her body always alert –
listening and fearing –
listening and fearing
Body tense – mind chattering
No sound sleep for days – nay even weeks – at a time*

*Chronic stress took its toll
The outpouring of Cortisol and Adrenaline –
known as the stress hormones – over a period of time
affected her body/mind/spirit*

*There was chronic fatigue – insomnia – irritability
All these and more*

*How could she get relief
How to turn off the hyper-alert
hyper-responsible switch*

*What am I to do – she thought
Then in silence she listened – shema
She listened for the wisdom that lay within*

*First she needed to restructure her time
so there was time – just for her – to be alone –
to take her own inward journey of
personal renewal and nourishment of the Soul
through meditation – contemplation – and prayer*

She needed to:
Become aware of her thoughts – her feelings
Confront her fears – her worries – her dreads
Become familiar with her inner allies and critics
and use her imagination and dialogue with these beings
Learn body/mind relaxation
Seek inner wisdom – guidance – compassion
Find her inner authentic power and courage
Learn how to treat herself as she treated her children
with loving kindness and patience –
even with gentleness and forgiveness

And guess what

Gradually her heart opened its loving arms to her
as she permitted Divine grace to enter –
bringing with it all kinds of gifts
including a major reduction of her chronic stress
with all of its destructive elements

Postscript

Years have passed
And now both of her children are grown
and – thank God – are free of asthma

And guess what –
the mother not only has a
beautiful relationship with her children –
she also has a beautiful relationship with herself

∞

Member of the Club

*I woke up one morning and thought
I was reaching the point of burnout*

*I was always on the go
Ever busy*

*I took on more duties
I was chronically tired – irritable – impatient*

I had trouble sleeping

*I woke up early thinking of all I had to do –
problems to solve - tasks to accomplish*

I felt agitated – my mind was ever busy

*I got up tired
and remained so throughout the day
I never felt joyful
and instead dwelled on things from the past*

*Like so many millions of others
I had joined The Club – whether I wanted to or not*

I was now a member of the Modern Age Stress Club

*The dues to this club are high and destructive
Yet I had been willing to pay them –
every day –
faithfully*

George W. Barnard M.D.

*To belong to this addictive group
I simply had to abide by four dictates:*

*I was not to believe in a spiritual world
because only the material reality existed*

*I was not to allow time
for my own inner nourishment
because I saw myself as being unworthy*

*I was to be a slave to the Ego
because no higher forces dwelled within me*

*And finally
I was to function almost exclusively in the
Sympathetic Nervous System fight or flight mode
because I did not know how to self-regulate efficiently*

*I did not know how to harness the power
of the Modern Myelinated Vagus Nerve –
the primary representative
of the Parasympathetic Nervous System restorative mode*

*So there was no harmonious balance
between these two great Autonomic forces*

*If I followed these four dictates
I was guaranteed
to feel as if I had no Soul –
or if I did –
it was parched dry
like an arid desert*

*Thus I was detached from and unrelated to God
yet I was afraid – no –
I was terrified to change*

I was miserable – yet I held onto my misery

*I feared if I let go – if I surrendered –
my world would disappear*

I would step into the abyss of the unknown

But then I took heart

*I decided that on my spiritual journey
I would take these first two steps –
I would get to know my Soul and
I would get to know my MindBody*

*In order to retrieve my Soul
I simply remembered my rich heritage*

*I am part of the Divine
My Soul was – and still is – a part of the Beloved
I let my Soul remember and awaken*

I decided to identify with Divine Self – instead of Ego

*I developed the necessary mystical relationship
between the Divine Self and the Divine Spirit*

*Now I give myself time each day
to till my internal spiritual garden
I discover the mysterious healing bounty
that is mine to harvest each day*

George W. Barnard M.D.

*In order to know MindBody
I see BodyMindSpirit as one unit –
really as one inseparable communication network –
because that is what it is*

*Through many millions of years of evolutionary process
human beings have developed this complex system –
but it can be understood*

*We can learn how to communicate with all parts
We can learn to self-regulate
so that all components
function harmoniously with each other*

*When we are able to master these skills
we are also better able to harness that wild one
we call chronic stress*

How do we do this

*First we have to understand our
BodyMindSpirit in its total evolutionary history*

*Humans were not sculpted anew
We were crafted on the frame of what worked well
for our primitive ancestors*

We still carry that frame with us today

*We have modified what we inherited
and have added new layers
with complex systems they did not have*

*But we still carry some of the components
of our primitive ancestors*

The issue then becomes:

*How can we access these hidden decision makers
How can we communicate with them
How can we assist them*

*This task becomes especially difficult since most of their
communication/regulation occurs at a non-conscious
level so that we are generally not aware of their existence*

*There are ways that we can communicate with the
decision makers – both verbally and non-verbally –
and assist in the regulation process*

*To do this we must learn their ways of being –
their ways of transferring information –
and how we can gain access to this data
and change outcomes*

*We know that this can be done
by entering a Meditative State through
meditation – visualization – imagination –
breathing – and touch*

*All these and more are within our reach as we
Practice – Practice – Practice*

∞

George W. Barnard M.D.

Coping with Stress

*Almost every day we will see it emerge in some form –
either in our own behavior or in someone we know*

*It shows up with expressions such as
"I'm stressed out"
"I'm having a bad hair day"
"I am about to melt down"*

*All of these are indicators of stress
and represent a painful time in our lives
The big question then becomes what sets off these events
and what can we do about them*

*First we need to realize that evolution has set
the stage by giving our brains a negative bias
so that we tend to predict the worst*

*This may be in the best interest of the species
but it is not good for our personal equanimity
because it causes us to be in a hyper state of readiness –
prepared to do battle or leave the scene*

*The research of Sonia Lupien as reported in her book
"Well Stressed" has shown that
there are four factors that lead to stress:
Novelty
Unexpected
Threat to Ego
Sense of not being in control
(Acronym – NUTS)*

*So the first thing we can do is to
pause and observe our internal state*

What is our BodyMindSpirit telling us

*We note our breathing – heart rate – muscle tension –
gut rumblings – feelings – thoughts – fears*

*Perhaps the most critical point to determine is
how our Ego is being threatened*

*But first – since we notice that we feel anxious –
let's do what we can to calm ourselves*

*Remembering the Modern Myelinated Vagus referred to
in Stephen Porge's book "The Polyvagal Theory"
we focus on our breathing patterns*

*Over and over we inhale deeply and
prolong the exhaling phase*

*This will activate the Parasympathetic Nervous System
and quieten our bodies*

*As Louis Cozolino mentions in his book
"The Neuroscience of Psychotherapy"
we can turn our eye gaze to the right to activate the left
hemisphere and the Orbital Medial Prefrontal Cortex
which will diminish the response of
the Amygdala to the perceived threat*

George W. Barnard M.D.

*At this point it is helpful to get rational assistance
from the left hemisphere and ask ourselves
"What is the wheat and what is the chaff
in this situation"*

*This will help us put things in perspective
and determine what is really important at this time*

*And finally we remind ourselves that
there are higher powers than Ego
on whom we can rely*

*We can find some peace during those times
when we are not in control of the outcome
by having faith/trust in this greater Force*

We take refuge and sing a song of praise

*"The Lord watches over the sparrow
and I know He watches over me"*

∞

The Dynamics of Stress

When stress comes – and it will –
do we know how to deal with it effectively

It seems as though more and more people are complaining
of being "stressed out"
but feel that there is little they can do about it

Let's review for a minute how stress is created

When we sense danger or feel threatened
then our bodies automatically react with
physiological – biochemical – psychological changes

If the threat is perceived as a major one then
the Hypothalamus in the brain kicks in
setting off a chain reaction in our body with the result
being an outpouring of the stress hormones – Cortisol
and Adrenaline – from the Adrenal gland

These chemicals trigger physiological changes –
our heart rate – blood pressure – breathing rate –
all increase – as does the blood flow to our muscles
and we have an extra amount of blood sugar for energy
All preparing the body for Fight or Flight stress reaction
(really a Threat – Challenge Defense System)

All this preparation assumes that our survival
is at stake and that the "other" is the enemy
and cannot be approached in friendship

This puts us in the position of being isolated and alone

What if there were a system in our body that was just the opposite of the Threat-Challenge-Defense System

According to Kerstin Moberg and Roberta Francis in their book "The Oxytocin Factor" there is a Calm – Connection System which produces an anti-stress reaction

This Calm – Connection System brings about a decrease in heart rate – blood pressure – and stress hormones (Cortisol and Adrenaline) and produces more effective digestion

At the same time it brings about a feeling of calmness and makes it easier for us to approach the "other" and be connected in friendship/intimacy

Our bodies are really wonderful – integrated – unified systems

While the sub systems that make up the unified whole are often moving in opposing directions – they usually end up reaching a balance between the opposing forces

In the ancient Chinese religion of Taoism there is the philosophical concept of Yin and Yang containing polar opposites that need to be balanced

Also in our own bodies we see a similar concept of opposite forces fulfilling their mission but through a process of balancing the internal forces with multiple systems

*For example both the Threat – Challenge System and the
Calm – Connection System contain components of the
Nervous System and the Chemical System*

*Within the Chemical System we have two peptides –
Vasopressin and Oxytocin – that are very similar in
structure yet quite opposite in function*

*Vasopressin is associated with the Threat – Challenge
System while Oxytocin is associated
with the Calm – Connection System*

*Vasopressin is thus part of the stress-producing
components of the body and Oxytocin
part of the anti-stress components*

*Both Vasopressin and Oxytocin are very ancient
chemicals in our body – even being present in prehistoric
animals prior to the development of a nervous system*

*They both function as Informational Substances that have
powerful effects on many components of our body*

*Oxytocin is our anti-stress factor that we definitely
need to understand when we become agitated or anxious*

*Or better still – even before we become upset
we need to connect with the calming and connecting
power of this marvelous chemical
The bottom line is that when the levels of Oxytocin
increase in our bodies then we are calmer
and want to be close with others*

George W. Barnard M.D.

*With knowledge and understanding
we can communicate with the Oxytocin System and
assist it in bringing about a release of this calming
chemical and thereby strengthen our
ability to influence our self-regulation*

*We can make contact with the decision maker
that controls the production and release of
Oxytocin in a number of ways*

*Imagination – visualization - light rhythmic touch –
exercise – massage – meditation –
breathing exercises – eating – sexual orgasm –
all of these are portals of entry
into the anti-stress system*

*By practicing one of these techniques we are able to enter
a Meditative State and communicate with our
non-conscious decision makers that control
the production of Oxytocin
But first let's look at Stress
What causes it
What dissipates it*

*As reported by Sonia Lupien in her book "Well Stressed"
there are four situations that bring about stress
Novelty
Unexpected
Threat to Ego
Sense of loss of control
All summed up with the acronym –* **NUTS**

*We also can do something about these four factors
that produce stress and assist our
BodyMindSpirit unit to deal with stress:*

Novelty
*If we can become familiar with the novel situation prior
to the time we actually have to confront it
then we will have some familiarity with it
and some ideas of how to adapt to it*

Unexpected
*While dealing with the unexpected – it often helps if
we turn inward – take several deep breaths – making the
exhalation phase longer than the inhalation phase*

*This triggers the Parasympathetic Nervous
System to help us calm down
At the same time it may be helpful if we attempt to deal
with this stressful situation as Observer-Witness Self
rather than Ego so that we have more objectivity*

Threat to Ego
*This is the most common threat that we encounter
This is because often the Ego tends to see the threat as
being more severe than it is or our Judgmental Self holds
us to a higher standard than we can realistically meet
Here it is helpful if we call on assistance from
Observer-Witness Self as well as Divine Self
to give us guidance and compassion*

Sense of Loss of Control

Again in a way this is a threat to the Ego and Ego acts as though the loss of control is a total loss

If we can do something that can signal Ego that we have some degree of control – even if it is focusing on our breathing – then we may feel less anxious

Our BodyMindSpirit Unit has a wisdom of its own in coping both with external and internal threats

As we gain more and more understanding of how this complex unit functions then perhaps we can learn more effective ways to communicate with it and find more effective ways to help respond to stress

∞

Learning to Let Go of Chronic Stress

Why is it so hard for me to learn how to let go of stress

*Almost every day I become aware
of repetitive behaviors that I am holding onto
that put me in a state of stress*

*And yet I stubbornly continue to grasp them
as if they were breaths of oxygen
that I need to survive*

Why can't I just relax and let them go

*To seek an answer
I begin a search of my many inner selves*

Which one is the culprit

*Who wants to be in complete control at all times
Who perceives threats when confronted with
novelty or the unexpected
Then the spotlight settles on one facet of self
EGO
Ego falsely believes that if it is not in control
it will not survive*

*This false belief can actually harm me because it can
activate a fight/flight response
in the ancient limbic system of my brain –
called the Amygdala*

*Whenever the Amygdala feels threated –
whether real or imagined – it responds with
a Sympathetic Nervous System body activation in
which there is an outpouring of
stress hormones – Adrenaline and Cortisol*

*These chemicals prepare us for a battle of survival
in which our body is prepared to
stay and fight or run away*

*Fortunately for us – as reported by Louis Cozolino in his
book "The Neuroscience of Psychotherapy" –
there is a more modern structure in the brain –
called the Orbital Medial Prefrontal Cortex –
that when activated – can counter the actions of the
Amygdala and thereby prevent or lessen the
Sympathetic effect and decrease the amount of
stress hormones released*

What can I do

*First I must move to a higher state of awareness
than the one in which Ego functions*

*As Observer-Witness Self I can think – feel – and act
in a more objective and rational way than I can as Ego*

*Ego generally functions at an impulsive level
and its ancient neuronal circuits are activated
from a fear base concerning my survival*

*Therefore as Observer-Witness Self let me remember to
call on the more modern evolutionary neuronal circuits –
namely the Modern Myelinated Vagus
and the Orbital Medial Prefrontal Cortex
to prevent a full blown fight or flight reaction*

*Let me first begin by communicating with the
Modern Myelinated Vagus studied intensely by
Stephen Porges and discussed extensively
in his book "The Polyvagal Theory"*

*I do this by initiating breathing exercises that activate my
Parasympathetic Nervous System which will
calm and restore my body to a peaceful state*

*I focus my awareness on my breath
I inhale a deep breath
I pause briefly
then I exhale slowly*

*With each inhalation
I stimulate the Sympathetic Nervous System
that prepares me for fight or flight*

*But with each exhalation
I stimulate the Parasympathetic Nervous System
which prepares me for calmness and inner peace*

*Gradually I learn to extend the time of exhalation and
thereby strengthen and prolong the Parasympathetic
activation and thus weaken or prevent the stress reaction*

George W. Barnard M.D.

*I then enter a Meditative State and request assistance
from the Orbital Medial Prefrontal Cortex
to quieten the Amygdala*

*In addition I learn other means of self-regulation in order
to integrate my many faceted inner components*

*I learn how to get Ego to share the decision making with
Observer-Witness Self and Divine Self*

These are higher components of Self than Ego

*They teach me how to live and function
from a higher state of being*

*They allow me to realize that
I am one unified BodyMindSpirit
They permit me to live in the Now*

*They teach me how to have compassion
for myself and for others*

*In essence they teach me Love
Love of Self – Love of the Other*

*If I am successful at self-regulation then I can
experience acute stress as a useful reaction*

*I can then let it go and not live in a state of chronic stress
where the stress hormones – Adrenaline and Cortisol –
will act in a destructive way on my BodyMindSpirit*

∞

Preventing an Emotional Meltdown

*Quite frequently we find ourselves
confronted with stressful situations*

*If we are not careful –
without our awareness or consent –
we will find ourselves in the midst of a storm*

*We need to know how to extract ourselves from the battle
before it becomes overheated*

What is the best way to do this

*First we need to become aware of
what our body is telling us*

*"Danger is near" our Amygdala cries out
When we hear this – we must listen – shema*

Next we label our situation for what it is

*As discussed by Louis Cozolino in his book
"The Neuroscience of Psychotherapy" if our Amygdala
is activated we are prone to overact –
so immediately we need to call on our
Orbital Medial Prefrontal Cortex for help*

*In order to do this –
while facing straight forward –
I gaze to the right
This will activate the rational left hemisphere containing
the Orbital Medial Prefrontal Cortex which will
balance the emotional right Amygdala*

George W. Barnard M.D.

Next I focus on my breathing

Since my Sympathetic Nervous System is already pumped up I need to balance it by activating the Modern Myelinated Vagal portion of my Parasympathetic Nervous System

In order to do this I take in a deep breath and prolong the exhalation so that it is longer than the inhalation phase

*I do this a few times
With each breath I allow my body to relax*

*Realizing that Ego can easily become threatened in stressful situations I decide that
I need to function from a higher state of Self –
as the Observer-Witness Self – and become emotionally detached from the heat of battle*

I still remain present but I am not threatened

*I am sufficiently emotionally removed that
I can see and think in a more objective manner*

*As I engage with the person who is emotionally charged
I begin to observe his/her body language
such as hand gestures and tone of voice –
but especially I look at the face – especially the eyes –
and try to figure out what message I am receiving*

The body language – which reflects the emotional right brain – may be giving me a different message than the verbal language which reflects the intellectual left brain

*I also pay attention to the messages that I am receiving
from my own body so that I can determine how tense or
relaxed I am about what is being said – and often
even more importantly – what is not being said*

*My body probably will be the best indicator of how my
internal Danger-O-Stat is registering a threat from my
internal or external environment to my Amygdala*

*If a threat of danger is assessed
then my body will prepare me to fight or flee
The important thing to determine is the
degree of threat that Ego is feeling*

*Many times there is no major threat
but Ego falsely believes there is a threat –
so we become super-charged and stressed out
when we don't have to be*

*To prevent us from responding to these false beliefs
we can implement preventive measures and
avoid paying the price of ongoing unnecessary stress*

*It will take patience to learn these new skills and it will
require practice and more practice to make these skills
a genuine part of ourselves*

*These skills – once acquired – will certainly support us to
lessen or avoid emotional meltdowns*

∞

George W. Barnard M.D.

Stress Burnout

*Sooner or later
all of us get to the point where we feel
we just can't give of ourselves anymore*

The teat has gone dry

*This is the time to turn inward –
experience a Meditative State – and
make contact with our inner beings*

*First – listen to our harsh internal critic –
Judgmental Self – which says:*

*You have not done enough
You should do more
Don't be a weakling
Don't be a coward
You ought not run away
You must be perfect*

Now listen to the voice of Divine Self – which says:

*Take several deep breaths
Become receptive – become focused – become centered
Stop doing and for a short time just be
Be gentle – especially with yourself – ahimsa*

*Remember those times
when you have had compassion for others
Now have compassion for yourself*

Unlocking Life's Secrets

*Remember those times when
your love and caring extended to others
Now let it extend to Thee*

*My treasure chest of vitality is always full
Come – rest your weary head on me*

*My forest is always full of silence
Come – put your tired mind to rest*

*My deep wells never run dry
Come – drink from my fountain
Let your parched Soul be wetted*

*My cupboard is never bare
Come - feast your spirit*

*You are part of me – I am part of you
Let yourself be nourished
Let yourself be*

*Which voice we listen to will
determine whether we become
depleted and barren
or
rejuvenated and full*

The choice is ours

∞

George W. Barnard M.D.

Sympathetic Nervous System Overload

*In our modern age of being on the go
there lies a hidden danger*

*When we keep ourselves going at such a fast pace
unknowingly we set our trigger point to fight at a level
where it does not take much to reach a boiling point*

*Before we know it – WHAM – our tempers flare and
off we go into a battle that we do not need*

Why is this so

Why do our minds and bodies react in this manner

*According to Stephen Porges in his book "The Polyvagal
Theory" it all goes back to our evolutionary heritage*

*Remember that in order to survive
evolution has geared us to perceive threats*

*When we perceive a threat –
whether it is real or imagined –
automatically and primarily out of our awareness
our brains prepare us to either
stay and fight or flee the scene*

*Either way our Sympathetic Nervous System
is activated and Adrenaline and Cortisol flow freely*

*Both of these stress chemicals are good for us
in the short term but can be deadly for us
if they persist on a chronic basis*

So why should they linger

*Because we continue to perceive a threat
even though it is not there*

*Our brain and body still produce the stress chemicals as
though we must still fight the tiger –
mammoth – or dinosaur*

*Normally after the acute threat is over
there is a feedback system that tells the brain and body
to stop the production of the stress chemicals*

*However if our mind still perceives danger –
real or imagined – it continues to command the brain and
body to produce the stress hormones – and they do*

This is a malfunction in our self-regulatory process

*When this happens we are on edge
We can feel uptight – worried –
anxious – and are unable to sleep well
or we can be grumpy – fault-finding – impatient –
or angry so that little frustrations become major and
we may lash out in a display of verbal or physical rage*

Well what – if anything – can we do

*Lots – so let us begin
First if we know that this can happen to us then
we can be watchful and catch it before we lose control
Usually we have body changes indicating
the presence of this process
Our body will give us clues if only we will listen*

George W. Barnard M.D.

*Our heart rate – blood pressure –
and breathing rate may increase
We may find ourselves sweating or have a dry mouth
The muscles in the back of our neck –
or elsewhere – may feel tight
These are all indicators of an increased Sympathetic
Nervous System stress activity and can be a signal for us
to bring in Parasympathetic Nervous System anti-stress
calming activity and get self-regulatory assistance
from our ally – the Modern Myelinated Vagus*

*Remember the breath
Recall that as we breathe in we activate the
Sympathetic Nervous System
and as we breathe out we activate the Modern Myelinated
Vagal portion of the
Parasympathetic Nervous System*

*So if we practice a deep inhalation and then prolong our
exhalation so that it is 4-6 times as long as the inbreath
we are calling on the Parasympathetic Nervous System
to calm and quieten our BodyMindSpirit unit
Remember we need to practice this daily for a few
minutes and not wait until we are already in a fight
before we call on it to help us*

*Besides learning and practicing this breathing technique
we can also discipline and balance our self-regulatory
processes with our daily time of meditation
to prevent this Sympathetic Nervous System
maladaptation process*

∞

Post-traumatic Stress Disorder (PTSD)

Many of us have heard about Post-traumatic Stress Disorder (PTSD) but just what is it

*Well it means that a person has had a traumatic experience(s) that has caused him/her to react to this threat/danger with painful emotional and/or physical symptoms that cause dysfunction in the victim
It also often causes distress in the family of the traumatized person as well*

A variety of symptoms may occur

Frequently the traumatized person keeps re-living the scene of the trauma in his/her dreams or in environments that have some element of the original scene – and that now trigger a fear/aggressive response in the body and behavior of the traumatized person

Keep in mind that the brain – over millions of years of evolution – has been geared to respond to threat/danger

*The brain does this by the use of ancient neural structures at a non-conscious level
so that we are not aware of the decision-making process until after the decision has been made
Even then we may only be aware of some physical changes – such as a racing heart*

Usually the BodyMindSpirit functions as an integrated unit

*However occasionally with trauma
that is severe or chronic –
some parts of the brain – such as the Amygdala –
will become so activated that other parts –
such as the Orbital Medial Prefrontal Cortex –
which are designed to counter and inhibit the
Amygdala – cannot sufficiently control it*

*When the Amygdala is not controlled a number of
systems influencing thinking – feeling – behavior
become dysregulated and the person can no longer
respond appropriately to danger*

*Even in the absence of danger his/her
BodyMindSpirit unit continue to act as
though a past danger is still present
In this suffering state he/she displays
a number of symptoms of PTSD*

*Because of the outpouring of Norepinephrine
the person is super-wired – hypervigilant – irritable–
anxious – and easy to anger*

*He/she may experience flashbacks
and act as though the past trauma
is in the present moment*

*Under the influence of an increased production of
Dopamine and Opioids the individual attempts to
defend him/herself against perceived dangers by
withdrawing and becoming isolated –
guarded – or suspicious of others*

*This behavior causes increased interpersonal/family
problems and interferes with the ability to hold a job
This in turn sets off a spiral of financial difficulties*

*Feeling depressed and sensing oneself as a failure there is
often an increase in suicidal thoughts and attempts*

*How are we best to understand this complex topic
and offer relief to the traumatized person*

*Peter Levine – the author of "Waking the Tiger" –
has worked extensively with
individuals suffering from trauma*

*He believes that in essence the suffering has occurred
because the person has become stuck in one phase
of a process dealing with threat*

*Stephen Porges in his book "The Polyvagal Theory" has
stated that from an evolution perspective our bodies have
developed a three level mode of responding to threat*

*On the first level the Modern Myelinated Vagus
responds by preventing an outpouring of the stress
hormones – Cortisol and Adrenaline*

*If this does not contain the danger threat then the body
goes to the next level with an activation of the
Sympathetic Nervous System which prepares
the body for a Fight/Flight response*

George W. Barnard M.D.

*And if this does not contain the threat and we feel
helpless and that we are going to die then the most
ancient system – the Ancient Unmyelinated Vagus –
is activated along with a Freeze /Feign death
(immobilization) response*

*Peter Levine in his book "Waking the Tiger" states that
he believes that the person suffering from PTSD
has become stuck in this latter mode
and his/her energy is frozen here*

*He writes that with a gradual therapeutic approach
the person can pass through this
"immobilization" phase –
complete the process of mobilization –
and experience recovery*

∞

Chapter 7: Relationships

Attunement

Sometimes even the most simple of our actions can have a profound effect on another human being

It happened to me recently

*I was standing at the counter
when she walked up to me –
touched my arm – and said*

*"You were able to listen to me – hear what I said –
and then take action – I appreciate that"*

*Now look at this brief interchange
Essentially it is a moment of attunement*

*How wonderful it is when we realize
that we have been heard*

*I think that attunement means so much
because we realize that we are not alone*

*Another being understands that we have needs
and is willing to seek ways of fulfilling them –
even if it is simply to acknowledge our existence*

*If we watch the interaction
of a mother and her infant
we see the wonderful power of attunement*

George W. Barnard M.D.

*It is as though the mother is scanning the infant
with all her senses in order to determine
exactly what the infant is trying to tell her*

*She looks at the child – especially monitoring
the facial expressions for meaning*

*She listens to the infant and
notes the quality of the sounds
Is there fear – pain – emotional discomfort*

*She touches her beloved offspring
Is there tension in the muscles
Is the skin hot*

*She smells her precious one
Does the upchuck smell sour
Is there poop in the diaper*

Note that all this is done to decipher the code

*Since the infant cannot communicate verbally
all this occurs on a nonverbal level –
and yet it is so effective if the caretaker
is attuned to the infant and his/her needs*

*The infant is unable to consciously remember these events
but you can bet your dollar that his/her
body holds them as implicit memories*

*These memories greatly influence the way the child –
and later the adult – views the world and even more
importantly – how she/he views herself or himself*

*Now what do you think happens when a
caretaker and child are not in attunement*

*You got it right
There are problems – major problems*

*This is where basic issues like trust have their origin
This is where we establish our sense of worth – of value*

*If we don't feel that we have been heard or
that our needs have been satisfied
we are out of attunement in our relationship*

How then do we re-establish attunement

*Or if we never learn this vital skill
what happens to our relationships throughout life*

*These early wounds can have profound influence on so
many of our interpersonal relationships*

*They also help to determine basic traits and qualities such
as our ability to feel compassion for another human or to
forgive when we have been wronged*

*I think that you can see why
so many marriages get screwed up*

But there is hope

Until the moment of death we can change

*And sometimes it begins with our ability to listen –
shema*

This is a good place to start

*We need to learn first how to listen to our self
and then how to listen to the other*

*Keep in mind that this type of listening
begins with learning how to listen to our body
and then carefully deciphering
what has been communicated*

∞

Complicated Families

*Sometimes it is hard to realize
just how complicated families can be
until we are part of such a family
Then we are painfully aware of it*

*For instance Molly and Joe have been
divorced for almost fifteen years
Their oldest daughter – Susan –
is getting married soon*

*Now the plot thickens
While they were married Joe was an alcoholic
and was physically abusive to Molly*

*Since their divorce Molly has wanted to have as
little contact as possible with Joe because of
all the bad memories she has of their relationship*

*Their children think that she should forgive Joe
and forget all the miserable times that she had with him*

*Molly has struggled for years
with the forgiveness process
and she certainly has been unable to forget*

*As the wedding approaches
Molly is becoming more and more anxious
because the abuse that she experienced from Joe
keeps intruding into her awareness
and even interfering with her sleep*

George W. Barnard M.D.

*She certainly does not want her anxious condition
to spoil the wedding for Susan so she decides
to contact her minister for assistance*

*The minister listens carefully to her story and
asks Molly if she feels pressure to forgive Joe*

*Molly says she does because
she has heard all her life that we should forgive
She has tried but her resentment and hatred
linger on – sucking her dry*

*The minister tells Molly that forgiveness is a process
that cannot be forced into a certain timetable*

*He wonders if Molly might be having problems
feeling compassion for herself for not being able to forgive*

*As soon as Molly heard the minister's words
she breathed a deep sigh of relief and said
"That is exactly what I have been doing"*

*As she sat back in her chair her anxiety seemed
to float gently from her body as she said
"I wouldn't ask another person to forgive on a certain
schedule and I will no longer ask that of myself"*

*She asked the minister for a closing prayer
After the prayer she walked out of the door
with a smile on her face*

*Ah – the power of compassion
Ah – the power of self-forgiveness and acceptance*

∞

Early Traumatic Relationships Impact Us

Young Isaac never saw it coming

His father had awakened him early that morning and told Laughter – this is what the name Isaac means – that they were going on a journey

What Abraham did not tell his son was that the night before he had heard a voice that he believed was God's voice

The voice told him to take Isaac – his only son – to a particular place and to sacrifice him as a burnt offering

Now there is no mention in the Bible that Abraham made any attempt to plead with God to save the life of his innocent son

But the Bible does mention that he had made such a plea regarding the lives of the innocent people living in Sodom and Gomorrah

We do not know why he did not make such a plea for his own young son

On their way that morning Isaac was curious and he asked his father "Where is the lamb to be sacrificed"

His father answered "God will provide"

George W. Barnard M.D.

Abraham built the alter and placed wood for the fire

*Terror must have engulfed Isaac
because at this time his father tied him
and placed him on the sacrificial altar*

*Abraham then raised the knife to kill his son
but before he could plunge the knife
the Angel of God called out to Abraham
"Stop! Lay down the knife!"*

*The Angel then commended Abraham
for placing God first and being
willing to sacrifice his beloved son*

*The Angel – speaking as the Lord – promised to make
Abraham a great leader of nations
because Abraham had obeyed him*

*But what about Isaac – the innocent –
but still intended victim
of this ancient need for there to be a sacrifice*

*What was he to do with the horrific memories
now deeply embedded in his brain*

*After this horrible experience could
he ever trust his father again*

Or for that matter could he ever trust anyone again

Could he ever relax and feel safe

We don't know if later
he would awaken with night terrors
screaming out in great fear
heart pounding as if it would explode
drenched in sweat
breathing rapidly
pupils dilated
as he relived this horrible experience
night after night

Always questioning – "Why me"
"When will my pain leave me"
but sadly never receiving an answer

From knowledge gained by working with
victims of severe trauma it is certainly safe
to say that these early traumatic events
and relationships wound us in a severe way

The damage to the innocent traumatized victim lingers
on and may show its destructive effects for a long time

Not infrequently the negative effects
are passed on to the next generation

But there is hope
Beliefs and behaviors can change

Each of us may ask the questions:
What do I think needs to take place
How would I go about making these changes

∞

George W. Barnard M.D.

Facing a Big Decision

She received a big shock today

*Her husband returned home from a business trip
He had startling news
The CEO of his firm had offered him
a promotion – a vice-presidency*

*He would be the youngest in the history of his company
He would receive a significant pay increase
Wow – what a compliment to him*

*He and his wife greatly appreciated that his bosses had
finally recognized his talents and his contribution
to the growth of the company*

*There was only one hitch –
to receive the promotion they must move from their
beloved Georgia to California*

What a blow

*They are well settled in their community
and have a network of valued friends
Their extended families are nearby
They love their home – their church –
their children's schools*

*They feel settled where they are
They feel blessed where they are*

*Now they feel torn
Their values will be put to the test*

They must now face who they are

What are the priorities in their lives
How will they sort it all out

How will they make the important decision

What will be their process

One thing is certain
They know they must talk
Talk openly – talk frankly
Share each other's hopes – dreams
Share each other's fears – dreads

And they do

They set aside time – just for the two of them –
as they open their hearts – their Souls – to one another

They look deep within
to search for guidance – for direction

As they make this critical decision
they have their love for each other –
they have their faith in a Higher Being

Together they will face this crisis

What they decide will not be as important
as the process –
the way they choose

George W. Barnard M.D.

Postscript

*And how did they decide
Well it wasn't easy but
they chose to remain in their beloved Georgia*

They looked at what really mattered in life

*Here was their family
Here were their friends
Here was their home*

*These are the people they cherish
This is where their values are*

They are so glad they chose as they did

∞

Getting Closure through Acceptance

*There he was – in the airport – waiting for his plane
All morning long he had been so rushed
he had not paused to assess his thoughts – his feelings*

*He was getting ready to travel South
to return to his beloved alma mater*

Will – his dear friend and mentor – was seriously ill

*His friends had told him that Will's condition
was deteriorating rapidly –
the time of his passing seemed close*

*As he sat in the waiting room
he closed his eyes – breathed deeply several times –
and let the visual scenes float before him as they saw fit*

*And there were many of them
– the first time he met Will – then his Dean
– the many occasions that the two of them had spent
alone sharing stories as only close friends can do*

*Over the years together they had spent many hours
together and their friendship deepened*

*But now it was coming to a new phase –
a letting-go phase
And this was not going to be easy
Feelings – sensations – thoughts – memories
all kept demanding to be noticed
And there was especially one that kept sneaking in*

George W. Barnard M.D.

*At first he wasn't sure what to call it
but then it became clear – its name was "dread"*

*Dread is that terrible feeling we all try to avoid
We sense something unpleasant is about to happen
but we feel helpless to stop it – we just have to wait*

*But wait a minute – perhaps he was not helpless
Instead of attempting to avoid dread – why not face it
Why not let into his awareness all that dread had to offer*

*Yes indeed he could be with Will
He could openly tell him all that
Will had done to enrich his life*

*He could share both his tears and his laughter
He could tell Will how he would cherish
the times they had together and that
the memory of these times would live on*

Or he could do none of this

*They could simply sit in silence or
perhaps just be in the present moment together
and carry on where they left off
the last time they were together*

*In any event love will certainly be present
and dread will no longer be there
Now there was calm acceptance
He was simply letting be*

∞

Him and His Old Dog

She looked out the window
and saw the two of them walking away –
him and his old dog

They would be gone hunting all day

Once again she was left alone to manage the kids
After all she was the mother – the wife
This was what was expected of her
Again and again

He brought home the money – at least the major portion

She too had a full time job
but somehow that didn't seem to count
She was the wife – the mother

Why couldn't he understand
Why couldn't he appreciate
Why couldn't he help
After all they were his kids too

What made matters worse –
at the end of the day he would come home –
expecting his dinner to be ready
expecting the kids to be in bed
expecting her to be available for sex –
even expecting her to enjoy it – to put away her pain –
her resentment and to turn on her body response
as she had done so many times before
But not today

George W. Barnard M.D.

She washed her tear-stained face
She called on her inner courage

Although still trembling
her muscles stiffened

As he entered the front door
he was greeted with the words

"We have to talk
Things have to change"

∞

Laboring to Bring Forth a New Creation

*I have often wondered –
Where was my Soul before I was created
in the womb of my earth mother*

*I have also often wondered
What was the essence of the universe
before it was created
in the womb of the Divine Mother*

*Was I planned – wanted – desired
Was the universe planned – wanted – desired*

*What labor of love did both my earth mother
and my Divine Mother endure to
bring forth her new creation*

*Was there joyful suffering – painful ecstasy
or simply agony with the wish for it to end*

*How did she/She feel in those brief moments
before birth when the pain of contractions
seemed to be more than she/She
thought she/She could endure*

And then there was relief – there was life

*There was new creation – her/Her creation
There was the universe – there was me*

*How did She feel at her first look at the Universe
How did she feel at her first look at me*

George W. Barnard M.D.

Was Mother God bonded to the Universe
Was earth mother bonded to me

Did either mother welcome her newborn
with a smile of joy

Then a new understanding revealed itself to me

The creative birthing of both the Universe and me
is a continuous evolving process

Through my choices I can influence changes in both
as I labor to bring forth a new creation –
as I become a birth mother
of a new me

∞

Letting Go

She accompanied him to his college dorm room
and then said goodbye

Oh how her body trembled
Her voice cracked as she said those words
"I'll call you tonight"

He replied
"I love you Mom – I will be alright"

This was a big moment in her life –
perhaps one of the biggest in nineteen years

Could it really have been that long ago –
when she first held him –
when she stroked his face
and thought how beautiful he was –
this only child of hers

Other first memories flood in
His first tooth
The first step
His first day at school
Driving a car alone for the first time
His first date
The first job

Now this first
His first real time away from home

College beckoned and he answered the call

George W. Barnard M.D.

But can she

*Can she take a deep breath
shed more than a few tears
and then let him go*

*Her head says she can
but her grieving heart has its doubts*

*This is a giant step for her
One that she has both longed for and dreaded*

She has put so much of herself into this mothering role

*And now as she turns and walks away
Suddenly she feels so empty – so alone*

*What will life be like without him
What will fill that void*

*In her heart – in her life –
no one ever told her it would hurt so much*

*And yet within – she knew
She has prepared herself for this moment*

*So she allows the pain to come –
to be felt – to be endured
At times it feels as though every cell in her body
individually insists on expressing its grief*

*But she allows the pain to come
She has suffered before
She is no stranger to loss – to grief*

*She knows that grief is like the day lily
here to share itself in this moment and then gone
perhaps to be replaced tomorrow by another
and it too shall fade*

*As she walks from the dorm she automatically
bonds with the strength of all the other mothers
who have walked through those doors –
knowing she has let go of her boy
so he may return a man*

*A painful but necessary step
She passes through the door and
sheds tears of sadness for her loss and
tears of celebration – of acknowledgement
for her role in raising this fine son*

Postscript

*A number of years have come and gone
Her son is grown up and married to a
wonderful and beautiful woman
And now they have a son of their own*

*Now she can be the grandmother
A new role – but she is ready
She knows in her heart
Her son is fine and so will be her grandson
She smiles to herself and feels joyful*

∞

George W. Barnard M.D.

Mammy

Have you ever had someone see you as being precious

*Have you ever had someone love you completely –
no matter what you did*

*Well I know someone that has
and she calls this beloved one "Mammy"*

*She gave her so many positive memories
and these still light up her heart*

*Some are even imprinted in her cells –
especially those cells in charge of her smell and taste*

*With these memories her taste buds awaken and her
saliva flows like a thawing mountain stream in spring*

*She sees herself walking into Mammy's kitchen
There stands Mammy with a big smile
and with a platter of her favorites –
steaming hot homemade biscuits
covered with butter and molasses
Yummy and yummy again*

Mammy – you filled her soul as well as her tummy

Now it is her turn to be "Mammy" and she loves it

And so do her children and grandchildren

∞

Midwife – Guide – Mentor

*She paused and looked out over the new group
She had been here before
but this time she became silent – and reflected*

*This was such a unique journey –
in fact a journey of the Soul
and she was to be for them*

*Midwife – Guide – Mentor
She would be the one to help them
find their way on this spiritual voyage*

*There would be pitfalls to avoid –
obstacles to overcome and of course if one seemed down
or even momentarily lost their way
she was there to comfort – console – encourage*

*She was to be a hands-on leader – healer
This meant she would share her real being –
her true emotions – her honest thoughts
She would be with them during
their doubts –
their denials –
their resistances –
their regressions –
as they struggled ever onward on their spiritual journey
to find who they were –
and who they might become*

George W. Barnard M.D.

For some she would be the family they never had
For others she would be the mirror
they always longed for
reflecting back to them their true being

On this spiritual journey – sadhana –
there would be both tears and laughter
but through it all there would be love – acceptance

She would be with them
for such a short time and
then she must let them go

Her heart both rejoiced and ached as she
anticipated her journey with her newfound friends –
who would soon become members of her spiritual family

She smiled and greeted them
"Welcome dear ones
Your journey begins NOW"

∞

Moments to Cherish

For years they have performed the same ritual each night
They take their baths and get in their PJs
Then they get in bed – hold hands –
and begin remembering good times together
They close their eyes – take in a deep breath
and then let it out slowly

He said to her "Tonight it is your turn to begin"
"Alright" she says "Let's go back to the first time we met
Let's visualize that time so that we can see ourselves
as we were then and feel as we did then"

As they relived that time they described aloud –
almost in a whisper –
the thoughts and feelings they were experiencing

They found it hard to believe the intensity
How alive they felt – how joyful they were

These were not just memories of the mind
They were powerful memories of the body

They were so real that it was
as though they were not memories at all
but were experiences of the present moment

And maybe – just maybe – they were and are
In any case – they cherished the moment
And so their nightly ritual continues
Ah such sweetness

∞

George W. Barnard M.D.

Now I am the Gardener

The night before he arrived back home
he did not sleep well

His mind was racing like an athlete in training
His feelings were bubbling like a rapid mountain stream

He had been asked to speak
at the funeral of a dear friend – a mentor

So many memories gushed forth
claiming their right to be heard

As he approached the podium he reminded himself
Breathe deeply – breathe deeply

Then he looked out at the faces
So many friends – so many loved ones

Their faces told him that he was accepted
His body relaxed and he began

As he told his story –
his journey with this beloved woman –
his love for her carried his tale
like a father carrying his child

Their friendship began when
he was only twelve years old

Unlocking Life's Secrets

*It grew from the size of a mustard seed
to that of a flowering tree
which bore fruit with the sweetest taste –
the fruit of values
the fruit of one's worth
the fruit of compassion
the fruit of giving*

All these fruits from a single tree

*She was an excellent gardener and she taught by example
She showed him how to plant with great expectations
She showed him how to nourish with tenderness
She showed him how to weed with vigor
She also showed him how to harvest with joy*

*He spoke his words of love
He spoke his words of appreciation*

*Then he realized now I am the gardener
Now I must teach by example*

*As he left the podium
he could almost hear her whisper
"Well done – well done"*

*Indeed she had taught him well
She had taught him through her being*

∞

George W. Barnard M.D.

Our Home is Special

*This is our home
How do I describe it*

*First with Pat at the center it is a place of comfort
Not just physical but emotional comfort too*

Certainly a base to which we may return again and again

*A retreat for withdrawal
when we need repair and healing*

*But most of the time a zone
to experience the joy of being together
as we mingle with loved ones
or as we share a delightful home-cooked meal*

*Favorites include:
Spaghetti and meatballs
Country-style steak with gravy and biscuits
Chocolate pie or banana pudding
and of course cornbread and milk*

*Home is where we celebrate special occasions
Birthdays – graduations – Christmas – weddings
Usually a play or song was written
to honor the one whose special day it was*

*Our home is always special
Filled with love and acceptance
Just remember – you are always welcome*

∞

Welcome Home My Son

*Our oldest son Bill approached his mother
and me with a broad smile on his face*

*"This is for you" he said as he handed Volume 1 of his
spiritual memoirs to each of us*

*I knew that this was coming
I just didn't know when*

I was filled with a mixture of joy and dread

*Joy because I knew where I was in
my relationship with him now*

*Dread because I was not certain what he would say about
the painful years of getting to this present moment*

*Although I didn't know it at the time Bill's spiritual
journey had begun when he was about 12 years old*

*I did find out about his spiritual journey with
considerable pain when he was about 20 years old*

*He had traveled to Europe to discover who he was and
subsequently dropped out of college after one semester*

*While overseas he had learned about a Guru –
a spiritual teacher – from India whose message
meant a great deal to him*

*He began to follow this spiritual path and
became an ardent devotee of the Guru*

Both my wife and I were threatened by this development

George W. Barnard M.D.

We experienced this action as being a danger to us
He expressed such intense love – loyalty – and devotion
to the Guru that we felt we had lost our child

I felt that my son had left our family and
become a member of another one

I was not sure when – or if – we would ever get him back

Both my wife and I went through a period of
grief and mourning over the loss of our son

In many ways we experienced it
as the death of a loved one

But then there was a resurrection

After about seven years Bill decided to return to college

And did he ever

First his undergraduate degree
then a Masters degree
and finally a doctorate degree in Religious Studies

He now teaches Comparative Religion
at a large university

Needless to say both my wife and I were
proud of him and his accomplishments

We were even more thrilled with the new and loving
relationship that we have with our son

We understood each other on a new level

There was less parent-child interaction
and more friend-to-friend relationship

*Reading his spiritual memoir gave us a different
perspective of his personal growth –
and of ours*

Bill's spiritual journey has been amazing and beautiful

*I know that for me seeing his transformation
has been inspiring and pleasing*

*I also know that the suffering I experienced as he went
through his transformation influenced me to turn inward
and set out on my own spiritual journey*

For this I am extremely grateful

*But most of all I am thankful for
the loving relationship that we have now*

Indeed – "Welcome home my son"

∞

George W. Barnard M.D.

Receiving The Bouquet

"These are for you" – the young woman said –
as she handed her bridal bouquet to the older woman
"You have been so nice to me
I want you to have them"

There was an audible gasp
She couldn't believe it
No one had ever done anything like this for her
She was almost overwhelmed

"They are so beautiful " – she said
"but I can't take the flowers – they are yours"

But reluctantly she did take them

The flow of love was so great that she simply allowed
herself to be carried away in a rush of joy

"Thank you" she whispered "I will cherish them"

As she held the flowers for her photograph to be taken
she had a renewal of spirit – of vitality

Almost feeling as she had fifty years ago
as she held her own bouquet on that
special day of special days

Ah – the power of love flowing in an ever endless circle
from one bride to another – from woman to woman –
kindling the flame of each Soul it touches

∞

Seeking and Receiving Blessings

*On bended knee
I approached my dying father*

*Father – I come before you
seeking your blessings on me – as I am
The blessings can come before or after you depart
But I request they come now to set me free – free to be me*

*And as a final gift
I request that you bestow on me that strength of yours
I cherish most – your chutzpah – your boldness*

*Oh what a treasure that would be –
an honor everlasting
A value which I can then pass on to my sons
in remembrance of your spirit*

*He nodded silently in assent and
laid his hand gently on me
"My son" – he said in a voice so clear –
"This blessing comes from my heart in the hands of love
carrying recognition of your worthiness – just as you are
Let it be the vessel of wholeness to contain my chutzpah
which I now pass on to you"
Our ritual of love ended
as I first pricked his finger and then my own
to mix our blood of acceptance
as our final farewell*

∞

George W. Barnard M.D.

Spring Ecstasy

*In former days not too long ago
because of our sacred rituals
they would have called us "The Wild Women"
or maybe even "The Witches"*

*Now other women just shake their heads in secret envy
and call us "The Joyful Seven"*

*Each spring we run away from home
and head for the beach*

Here there are no husbands – no children – no demands

*For a few brief nights we are free
Free to do as we want and just be –
without demands from anyone*

*We get up when we desire
We go to bed when we wish
and in between we have a ball*

*Sometimes we walk the beach alone
Other times we sing and dance together*

*We may wear old clothes and
go without makeup for days*

*Then again we may put on that new outfit
and prance about the house
as though we were on a modeling stage*

But always there is joy and laughter

Well maybe not always

*There are precious moments of sharing
and holding one another
as we let go of the pain we have carried in silence*

*As the tears flow and relief comes
we know once again the blessings of sisterhood*

We return to our homes feeling renewed and replenished

Ah – Spring Ecstasy

I can't wait

∞

George W. Barnard M.D.

Standing on the Shoulders

*Most of us have someone who has been such a big
influence in our lives that we can literally say
"I stand on the shoulders of that person"
An example of this took place just recently*

*Will – the former dean of a university –
was terminally ill*

Word of his impending death spread like wildfire

*Former students came from all over the country –
they just had to be there*

He had meant so much to so many

*Will was too weak to talk much
but he was still able to listen*

And boy did he listen – shema

*It seemed like there was a steady stream of
folks in and out of his room*

*Each one telling Will in his/her own unique way
just how much he had meant to them*

*Tears flowed freely as did laughter
Indeed it was a celebration of life*

*The nurse taking care of him said that she had never seen
such an outpouring of love in her entire career*

And now each one returns home

With time to think
Time to ponder
And time to rejoice

As the thoughts and feelings flowed freely
like a rapid mountain stream
each had opportunity to examine in detail
just how Will had shaped their lives
and to give thanks for the strong base he had provided

Now each one can now say
"Indeed I will miss him but
through me Will's spirit lives on
Now I can have broad shoulders
on which others can stand"

∞

George W. Barnard M.D.

Endorphin Bursting Into Glee

*The alarm clock went off
and they both seemed to hit the floor at the same time
Excitement was in the air*

*The sun was playing peek-a-boo with them
as it rose across the Vermont mountain
There had been a fresh snow during the night
They knew what awaited them on the ski slopes
Hurriedly they grabbed a cup of coffee
put their ski-gear in the car – and they were off*

*The air was brisk - it almost tasted fresh
This was their favorite time of the year
Even their muscles were becoming taunt
as they remembered the thrills awaiting them*

*The ride up the ski slope was fun
but their real joy was yet to come
"Here we go "they called
as they headed down the mountain*

*With each twist and turn of the decent
the endorphin release gave them a burst of glee*

*The air was cold and crisp
but the sun was bright and warm – just tingly right
As they reached the bottom of the run
they looked at each other – smiled – and said
"Could life be better than this"*

∞

In My Footsteps

*I looked behind
and saw my son
following in my footsteps*

*Only now he wasn't walking in the snow
he was journeying in real life*

*Only now my son wasn't four –
he was forty*

*Only now it wasn't a pretend game –
it was a deadly game of self-destruction*

*As father I had been a role model and
my son had followed my values*

But some of them were simply the wrong values

*I had lost balance in my life
The material world was valued highly
The spiritual world was valued little*

*This meant valuing the wrong things –
I excessively valued wealth and prestige*

*In the process I had become a workaholic
and so had my son*

*I had become a slave to Judgmental Self
and so had my son*

*I had lost contact with my Soul
and so had my son*

*I had lost zest for life
and so had my son*

George W. Barnard M.D.

For some time I was in agony

*Finally my denial gave way to suffering
so I began my inner sadhana – spiritual journey*

*I had made some progress on this journey –
or so it seemed to me
But was I up to this new challenge*

*Now my son was suffering
He was in his own crisis –
his own dark night of the Soul*

*How could I help my son
What was I to do – to be – for my son*

*First I could acknowledge
that I knew my son was hurting*

*I couldn't magically take away the pain
but I could affirm that the pain was real*

*I could reassure my son
of my willingness – my commitment –
and my availability – to share with him
knowledge – insight – and feelings
from my own spiritual quest*

*I could share what I had learned
about my own inner world:
my strengths – my weaknesses
my goodness – my meanness*

*I could admit and take ownership of those areas of
fatherhood in which I had not been good enough –
those areas in which I had missed the mark*

*I could acknowledge that I had not lived a balanced life –
and that I had set the wrong example*

*For these wrongs – and others –
I could ask forgiveness from my son*

*But mainly I could tell my son how much I loved him –
how proud I was of him*

*And whether there was a crisis or bliss
I would walk the path with him*

*I wouldn't always be there externally
but spiritually I would always be by his side
Cheering him on
Comforting him*

*Always reminding him of his worthiness –
of his inner sacred essence*

*Always reminding my son
of the eternal love I have for him*

Postscript

*It has been a number of years
since this poem was written
And I must tell you that all is well
between my son and me*

*We both benefited from that dark night period and
have both grown in our spiritual lives
We have regained contact with our Souls and with that
came a newfound purpose in our lives*

*At this time we have a wonderful relationship
and love our time together*

∞

George W. Barnard M.D.

Unfolding Into Wholeness

*In my journey through life
there has always been a void*

*You are the Thou
for whom I have searched*

*So take my hand
Take my heart*

*Let me unfold into the wholeness
for which my Soul has longed*

*Come be my Partner
through the rest of my life's journey*

∞

A Stranger No More

It seemed like such a beautiful autumn day

The fall colors were just beginning to arrive
It all seemed so peaceful

Then WHAM
Out of nowhere that pickup truck came
broadsiding their car
ramming the passenger side where my friend sat
crushing the door – pinning him inside the car
He knew only confusion – he felt only panic

He saw only a stranger
A large man with tremendous hands
A man with a calm – reassuring voice
"Just sit still Mister – I will get you out"
And he did – with such ease – pulling the metal apart
as though it was straw – instead of steel
Lifting my friend gently from the tangled mess

Once out of the wrecked car – my friend's head cleared
He could think straight once again
He turned to thank the stranger
but he was nowhere in sight

Then my friend thought
"Was that a stranger – or my guardian angel"
His head will never know but his heart is quite certain
In his heart there is only gratitude

∞

Chapter 8: Living a Full Life

A Model of Love

*If we stood at a distance and watched her
we would have thought
she was just a woman doing her hobby*

But no – she was much more

*She was a woman on a mission – a sacred mission
A mission of love – the agape kind of love –
unconditional love*

*She was giving herself to a higher cause
She was building family –
as she always had – by giving of herself*

*Earlier she did it by preparing wonderful meals
or having a welcoming home*

*Now she was doing it with her
beautiful counted cross stitch works of art
Each piece requiring tens or even
hundreds of hours of careful handcraft*

*Day after day and night after night she toiled
Stitch after stitch after stitch
Each carrying a bit of her
And each carrying a lesson to us of
what love really means*

*Patience – Perseverance – Diligence
Certainly these –
and more*

*Mainly she taught us about unselfishly
giving of self for a higher cause –
the building of a strong loving family unit*

And that she did – one stitch at a time

∞

George W. Barnard M.D.

Enjoying the Joy

*He and his wife burst into the room
"Guess what Mom" he said
"We are going to have a baby and it's a boy!"*

*The endorphin of all three flowed freely
from springs deep within their bodies*

*Their smiles seemed to spread from ear to ear
Their eyes beamed with gladness*

*For a brief moment there was silence
Then all three embraced
as their hearts beat in synchrony
and tears of happiness danced a jig*

*Could there ever be a greater time of happiness
She – like they – had dreamed of this occasion –
had prayed for this day –
and now it was here*

*She was going to be a grandmother
for the very first time
The longing of the past was now
the joy of the moment*

Could life be sweeter than this

∞

Fears from Childhood

*It is amazing to me
Amazing to see how defensive I can be
I do it with denial – avoidance – intellectualization
At times I even do it through
what I remember and what I forget*

*Sometimes I am aware of my defensiveness –
other times I am not
My guardedness has become such an
ingrained pattern of mine*

*Why so strong – why so powerful
Then I hear a small voice from within
"Ask the implicit memories of the unconscious
to share their secrets"*

*And they do – with Child Self speaking
"I am afraid that if I am open/unguarded with you –
you will see me as being vulnerable –
you will hurt me – you will control me
But an even deeper fear – you will abandon me"*

*These are all old childhood fears
Can I ever face them – dialogue with them
Can I ever begin to let them go
And then again from deep within
I hear the soft voice of Shekhinah
"You just did my child– you just did
Ahimsa – Ahimsa – Be gentle – Be gentle"*

∞

George W. Barnard M.D.

Accepting Nurturance from the Soul

*When I know how to accept nurturance from my Soul
then my addictions fall away
like a snake shedding its old skin*

*I no longer need that high from daily stimulants of coffee
or tea – that extra food – that striving for perfection*

*My frenzied addiction to time is lost
so I no longer have to hurry from place to place*

*My addiction to pleasing others is gone
I have an inner calmness
that buoys me through life's storms*

*My addiction to fear is no more –
even my fear of the great enemy – death
I feel secure in knowing my Soul is eternal
and will nurture me forever*

*How do I receive this nurturance
that is life's secret nectar*

*I simply roll away the stone
covering the entrance to my empty tomb*

*I become open and receptive to the love that my Soul –
sometimes called the Goddess of Love – offers me*

*This healing elixir then flows freely throughout my
being – bringing me healing – bringing me happiness*

∞

How Memories Influence Us

*As I walked out of the store he approached me –
his clothing was old and dirty –
his face was unshaven –
he appeared saddened as he walked toward me*

He had targeted me and I knew it

*My danger defense went on guard
I quickly tried to assess the level of danger*

He began to speak before he was close

*"I don't want your money" he said
"Today is Mother's Day
and I can't afford to buy her a gift*

*Could I get you to go to the store
(pointing to one nearby)
and buy something for her
I am the black sheep in the family
but I want her to know I care"*

*There were tears in his eyes
and his voice cracked as he spoke*

*This is an unusual approach for a handout
I thought – so I kept looking at his face – especially his
eyes – to see if I could trust what he was saying at all*

*I listened and he kept talking
I took several steps back to gain space
I tried not to let my fear show*

George W. Barnard M.D.

"Just a minute" – I said
"Let me put my package in the car"
all the while monitoring his body language
to assess his intent

"I don't have enough for a gift for your mother"
I said as I handed him a couple of dollars

He said "Thank you" and quickly walked away
I sat in my car for several minutes to see what happened
He soon reappeared and was trying to
determine who to approach next

As I drove away I tried to figure out why I acted as I did

I suspected that he was conning me
but somehow that wasn't important at the moment

Something about the encounter touched my heart
and my memory quickly led me back to several past
events – all dealing with compassion

My family was poor and after my father died
on several occasions neighbors brought in food
They didn't have to but they did

Later as I was heading off to college
members of my church collected a "love offering" for me
They didn't have to but they did

About the same time a woman I hardly knew
gave me some clothing that belonged to her husband
who had been killed in the war
She didn't have to but she did

*None of these memories were in my
conscious memory as I gave the man money
But their influence was there –
whether I was aware of it or not*

*In the past compassion had been shown to me and
today I showed compassion
I didn't have to but I did*

∞

George W. Barnard M.D.

Becoming Aware of Love

*It took me becoming aware of the love
that I have for my own children
to finally realize
how much love God has for me*

*It was becoming aware of this human love
that allowed me to become aware of Divine Love*

Or was there ever any difference

Maybe I was just slow in becoming aware of love

*But I am glad I did become aware
Glad that I am aware*

Even Now

∞

Hungry for the Beloved

Are you hungry for the Beloved
Are you hungry for the Beloved

Come run to the Lord

He's awaiting for you
He's awaiting for you

Does your Soul feel parched and dry
Does your Soul feel parched and dry

Come run to Spirit

She's awaiting for you
She's awaiting for you

Come feast at the Fathers table
Come feast at the Mother's table

Sing praises to his holy name
Sing praises to her holy name

Hallelujah
Hallelujah
Hallelujah
Hallelujah

∞

George W. Barnard M.D.

Let Us Open Our Hearts

*Come people come
Let us welcome Divine Spirit*

*Come people come
Let us welcome Divine Spirit*

*Let us open our hearts
so that Love may enter*

*Let us permit Source to be present
and guide our healing*

*As we open our hearts Love follows
and flows ever so gently through our bodies*

*Love – yes Healing Love – fills every cell of our being
All we have to do is to be relaxed - trusting and receptive
As we do we experience Grace –
yes we experience mysterious Grace*

*As Love permeates our being
we feel ourselves restored
No longer lonely
No longer alienated*

Just restored and whole – Just restored and whole

*We are one with Love
We are one with Spirit
This is Bliss – yes precious Bliss*

∞

Unlocking Life's Secrets

She Still Has the Memory

*She stood on the balcony
and looked out over the lake*

*Her memories carried her back almost fifty years
Was it really that long ago*

*She stood on the stage in New York City –
her voice ringing out
the words and sounds of South Pacific
Oh the thrill – the rapture*

*She catches herself humming – even mouthing the words
She can almost remember how they tasted in her mouth
Her diaphragm automatically contracts
to expand the lungs
Her larynx tries – but somehow is limited – as it strives
to recapture the shape needed to bring forth the sound*

*Then there is a tear in her eye
She knows so well – it is gone – gone forever –
that moment of her youth that was – but is no more*

*Then she smiles and walks away knowing so well
She still has the memory – hers to keep*

∞

George W. Barnard M.D.

The Power of Compassion

Let me lift my veil –
open my heart – to see – to feel – to understand
the pain and suffering of the Other

It is my compassion that has the power
to link my Soul with the Soul of the Other –
to taste the tears of her sorrow
to tremble with her fear
to embrace her loneliness
to be the willing recipient of her anger
even to forgive her when she has offended me

Why compassion
Because I care for her Soul and for my Soul

My compassion is for my Soul as air is for my lungs
or food is for my stomach
It sustains life – it nourishes the heart

But for me learning to be compassionate
has not been easy
Why has this been so

Because I was too wrapped up in my own Ego
and Ego just couldn't do it

I first had to experience a part of me –
Divine Self – that could feel with the Other
really become attuned to the Other

*This part could understand the mind of the Other
but in order to do this I had to become very familiar
with the body language of the Other*

*It was not so much what was
being said verbally in words
Instead she sent the message through
the tone – the pitch of the voice –
and the rhythm of the delivery*

The non-verbal could be trusted more than the verbal

*I also focused intently on the message that
was being sent by the eyes of the Other*

*It was especially the message being sent by
the facial muscles and the eyes of the Other
that somehow communicated
the content of the Soul of the Other*

*It was here that I could receive primitive
messages of distress sent by the Other*

*And when I received them
my heart opened with empathy – with compassion*

Mothers do this naturally all the time with their infants

I was just a slow learner

But better late than never

∞

George W. Barnard M.D.

The Origins of Love

*In the Bible we are told that
God loves us and has from the beginning*

We are also told that we were made in God's image

*Both of these statements are pretty powerful
and until recently both concepts
have remained a mystery*

*But now while science can't talk much
about God's image
we are beginning to get a better understanding of love
so let's have a look*

*As humans when we are infants
our very survival depends on our basic needs
being met by someone other than ourselves*

*Some animals are self-sufficient soon after birth
but not humans*

*Our undeveloped bodies – brains – and minds
demand a long period of dependency
Years – even decades – are required for humans to
develop fully into the complex beings that we become*

*It looks like God and/or evolution has lent a helping hand
in establishing the bond between the
human infant and the mother/caretaker*

*When the baby is expelled from the womb at birth
the hormone Oxytocin is elevated
in the bloodstream of the mother*

*This ancient hormone not only aids in the strength of the
contractions of the uterus to bring about the birth
it is also the chemical that establishes the initial
attachment bond between mother and infant*

*In an unknown way Oxytocin stimulates the mother so
that she has feelings of love toward the infant –
so that she desires to care for her newborn child*

*Throughout the pregnancy there has been a bond
developing between mother and child
This bonding process increases dramatically after birth
because there now is a two-way communication system
intact between mother and infant –
with the child's behavior actually eliciting
love responses from the mother*

*Much of this two-way communication is done
at a non-verbal and sub-conscious level*

*After delivery – or maybe even before – there is an active
on-going signaling taking place between the two parties*

*The infant is communicating his/her needs and
the mother is receiving these messages and is responding
to meet the needs of the infant*

*Hence the transmission of love by the mother
and the development of trust in the infant*

George W. Barnard M.D.

*This link between love and trust is extremely important
and it will be evident in all future
relationships that the child develops*

*This applies to love-trust relationships between humans
as well as relationships between human and the Divine*

*What is equally important is that the bond that is
established between mother and infant
sets the tone for all other relationships*

*This early bonding is like a lens or filter through which
the later relationships will flow and be perceived
This early bonding affects the way we perceive ourselves
as well as how we perceive the Other*

*In this mother-child relationship the mother will be the
one that will be the one making an assessment of
what the child needs at any particular time*

*If enough of the child's needs are sufficiently met in a
timely fashion this will facilitate the child's ability
to develop a sense of trust in the Other*

*This assessment on the part of the mother is a complex
and difficult task and is more readily accomplished if the
mother is able to function from a "We-centric" rather
than an "Ego-centric" (i.e. "I-centric") position*

*This is because in so doing
she operates on a higher state of being as
Observer-Witness Self or as Divine Self
rather than as Ego Self*

*In so doing she will be able to assess the
needs of the child more realistically
and also to be more understanding – loving –
and compassionate toward her child*

*A mother's ability to function as Divine Self will permit
her to show her love as "agape" – unconditional love*

*And oh what a gift that is
because agape love is received by the child as
"I am being heard – I am being accepted as I am"*

*This means there is attunement
between mother and child
This early attunement paves the way
for later attunement with others*

*Experiencing it facilitates our ability later to attain
attunement with our spouse and with God*

*We are capable of experiencing this early attachment
bond because we are "hard-wired" to do so
Somewhere in the evolutionary history
this development aided survival of the species*

*Or it can be interpreted as from the beginning
God has loved us and set the necessary conditions for us
to be capable both of being able to love and be loved*

*Either way being capable of loving and being loved
is a wonderful experience –
so enjoy it*

∞

George W. Barnard M.D.

Two Basic Needs

*We all have two basic needs
The need to know and
the need to feel known by the Other*

*So simple – yet so powerful
Some might say it in another way –
the need to do and the need to be*

*Or perhaps it all goes back to
Yin and Yang
the ancient Chinese duo of complementary forces
active – passive
giving – receiving
male – female
night – day*

*We go around in a circle and we come back home
There is you and there is me*

I need to know myself – I need to feel known by you

*Sunrise – Sunset
The invisible whole*

*Life goes on
So do we*

∞

The Power of the Heart

When I open my heart to love
I feel my being expand without limits

How large can it get
Can there ever be an end

The boundaries between me and Thee disappear
like the merging of two streams
into one river flowing to the sea

Who is the Other
Who is Me becomes who is We
As I nourish you – I nourish me
As I deprive you – I deprive me

Love cannot be contained
It is the energy of the Universe
It is the power of the heart

A power without beginning
A power without end
A power available to you
A power available to me

O heart of mine open today
O heart of mine open wide

Let love flow – Let love expand

∞

George W. Barnard M.D.

Gratitude

*How can we express it to you
How can we tell you how appreciative we are
for all that you have done for us*

*Lately – as we have experienced our stressful time –
negative emotions have seemed so frequent*

*But this positive emotion of gratitude
lifts us to an amazing high*

*Our endorphins flow with such force and so much power
Every cell in our bodies is rejoicing
Each cell says "Yes – now it is my turn"*

*At this moment we can identify
with all who have been prisoners but now are free*

*We can also identify with a young woman
who has just delivered her first child –
looks at her baby's face – smiles – and says to herself
"Indeed the pain was worth it"*

*We have gone through a painful process together
and we have become stronger*

*Indeed we have become more thankful –
more appreciative – to God and to all of our family
and friends for all their support and assistance
in this painful process*

Indeed we are grateful – so thank you

∞

Gestation of the Love Child

*Daily she tended to this work of art
as though she were carrying the love child in her womb*

*She could not have been more diligent in her care
After all she knew what this piece of cross stitch
would mean to her daughter and son-in-law*

*The two of them had spent hours searching for
just the right picture for her to create
And they had found it
Their choice even had special symbolic meaning to them*

*Now the period of gestation was in her hands
Not a day went by that she did not carry out
her acts of nourishing love*

Each stitch was placed in just the right position

*There were 64 different colors
and each thread had to blend in a
harmonious manner with its neighbor*

*During the early days it was difficult to
see any signs of progress
Then slowly forms began to emerge
so that signs of life came into being*

*Gradually it was like viewing a
fetal ultrasound in multicolor*

George W. Barnard M.D.

*The concern of the artist though was
whether she could finish this work in time
She knew that it – like a pregnancy – could not be rushed*

*Time was essential for every component
to reach its required maturity*

*The necessary acts of patience and perseverance
seemed to flow naturally from her open heart
and they paid off handsomely*

*Finally she was able to say proudly
"That's it – let's take this baby to the framer"
And she did*

*Then daily she waited in silence
for the time she could share her joy with her daughter
and that time did come*

*On Christmas day the wrapping was lovingly removed
For a moment eyes were focused on the picture
and then on each other*

*As the two women embraced
the tears that flowed oh so freely didn't seem to know
whether they were tears of love – of gratitude – or both*

*But the soft words heard seemed so clear
"Woman - I love it and I love you so much!"
And each time in the future as she looks at this lovely
creation she will remember the words of its creator –*

"Remember you are well loved"

∞

Chapter 9: Death

The Final Letting Go

On my spiritual journey
I have had loads of experience learning to let go

There has been a tremendous struggle
With grasping
With clinging
With control

And now I face the final letting go

Will it continue to be
a fight
a holding on

Or will it be
a gentle unfolding

To assist me
I turn to my core – my breath

I follow Prana – my life breath

I take in on the inbreath
I let go on the outbreath

∞

George W. Barnard M.D.

Dealing with My Mortality

*It seems to me that in the past year
I have lost many friends
to death*

*Their lives dropping like
leaves from a tree in the early fall
bringing me once again
to deal with my own mortality*

*I feel as though I am running out of time –
wondering if I will change soon enough*

*Will I ever get to the point where I can
openly feel – openly show – my love*

*Where I can let my love flow from me
uninhibited by my fears –
so I can let it pour forth freely
like bubbles blown from a child's pipe*

*Bringing forth
joy
liveliness
playfulness*

I don't want to cheat death

I only want to celebrate life

∞

Facing Death Without Fear

*Whether I stand on the bow of the Titanic
as it sinks to the bottom of the ocean*

*or I am on the top floor of the World Trade Center
as it topples to the ground*

*or I am in the gas chamber at Auschwitz
as the deadly fumes surround me*

*there is always an inner voice reminding me –
"Fear not my child – I am with you"
Tat tvam asi – Thou art that
You are and forever will be*

*This voice gives me strength to be
This is a strength that is hard to understand
but so reassuring to experience*

*It says that even when my body exists no more
I continue to be*

*It says that the essential me – my Soul – is eternal
It cannot be destroyed*

*Knowing this – I now know how to deal with fear
I simply face it
See that it is a creation of my own making*

One part of my brain – the Amygdala – may make fear

*But another part – the Orbital Medial
Prefrontal Cortex – can take away the fear*

Fear has no power over me unless I give it power

If I am successful in reaching balance between the Amygdala and the Orbital Medial Prefrontal Cortex then the fear of death exists no more

It too has lost its sting

Even in death I continue to be

I simply transform to another form of being

∞

Goodbye Dear Friend

*Since you passed so suddenly – so unexpectedly
I didn't get a chance to say goodbye*

*I didn't get a chance to say
how much you meant to me*

We have known each other for such a long time

*Through all those years I appreciated your kindness –
I appreciated your understanding –
but most of all I appreciated your acceptance –
your acceptance of me just as I was and am*

*When I was with you I didn't have to pretend
I didn't have to wear a mask – I could just be me*

*Me with all my faults – even me with my shadow
That too was okay*

*Oh how comfortable that acceptance was
And yet how easy it seemed to be for you*

*Perhaps that was your special gift
It wasn't just with me because
I saw you do it with others too
Yet to each of us it must have seemed so special*

*Now although you are gone
I still experience your spirit lingering close*

And Friend – your acceptance lingers too

∞

George W. Barnard M.D.

I Knew Him So Well

He was with us
He was among us
and now he is gone
but somehow his Essence lingers on

He was so simple
Yet so complex

Always on an inner spiritual journey
Seeking to learn more about himself

Deeply rooted in family and home

Full of loving kindness
yet speaking with a direct tongue
so you knew where he stood

Always acquiring new ideas
at the same time letting go of the old

Pushy – impatient – trying to get his way
Accepting – tolerant – looking out for the Other

Would these opposites never merge

Yet somehow they expressed his wholeness
All these qualities and more – you may add

After all you too can say
"I knew him so well"

∞

The Aftermath of Death

Since the death of his beloved wife
his sleep has been quite disturbed

His thoughts just keep churning
like a motor stuck in high gear

This morning the sun is not yet up
but he has tossed enough

He crawls out of bed and sits on his front porch

The fog has rolled in
That's the way his mind feels – foggy

He sits in his favorite rocker – closes his eyes –
and watches his thoughts roll by
like a movie in slow action

In all of his life he has never felt more out of it

Things just don't seem real
Nothing makes sense

When will it all end
Indeed will it all end

He feels so empty
So alone

But wait a minute
What is that he hears

George W. Barnard M.D.

*There had been silence
but off in the distance
he hears the morning dove*

*As he focuses his attention
there are other sounds*

*The birds – the frogs – the train whistle –
all reminding him that life is nearby*

Now the sun is up and the fog is moving out

*For some strange reason he feels comforted
and even a little bit hungry
So he goes inside for some breakfast*

∞

Sweet Words Lingered On

Before she left her driveway her tears were flowing freely

Oh how she dreaded this trip
She knew what was ahead
Just not when it would come

Her best friend was dying from cancer and
she wanted to be with her when the end came
Finally she arrived at her friend's home
The two dear friends greeted each one another
with smiles – tears – and warm embraces

"I'm so glad you came" her friend said
"Because I'm leaving – hopefully today or tomorrow"

Then after a brief pause "I need your help –
I want to write a letter to my 2 year old granddaughter
Could you get me the pen and stationary"

Although love flowed freely from her ill friend's heart
the effort had exhausted her

So she climbed into bed with her friend and held her hand
Her friend seemed to relax and whispered
"Let's go to the beach – let's go walk on the beach"

There was a gentle sigh – followed by silence –
The end had come for her friend but
sweet words lingered on
"Let's go to the beach – let's go walk on the beach"

∞

George W. Barnard M.D.

Journey Called Mourning

*They had been married for 52 years
And now she is gone – or is she*

*Her body is no longer here but her spirit certainly is
He thought they talked a lot while she was alive
Now he thinks perhaps they talk even more
They talk – they laugh – they cry
They relive experiences –
experiences that are so comforting –
so meaningful for him*

*Still there are bad times – lonely times –
especially when he goes to bed
He reaches out to touch her face but she is not there
So he opens himself –
opens himself to feel his emptiness – his loneliness
Really he opens himself to feel his suffering*

*Then the paradox begins
The more he opens himself to feel his pain
the more he opens himself to feel his fullness*

*It is then the other memories flood in
to nourish his parched psyche
He recalls her laughter – he remembers her smile
All images – powerful images
Images to maintain him – to heal him –
on this journey we call mourning*

∞

Goodbye Friend – Hello Angel

My friend has gone and now I must say goodbye

*I saw how you suffered on your journey
What a task it was just to get the body
to carry you through the day*

*I know of your long nights in which
you searched in vain to get a whiff of relief*

*Through it all you carried on so well –
trying so hard to maintain that friendly smile –
so full of joy*

*And now that you are gone
how do I deal with your absence*

*I look at the mystery of it all
I feel empty – yet there is a fullness
I feel a loneliness – yet there is your presence*

Maybe it is a mystery no more

*You simply have become my guardian angel
and will journey by my side forever*

∞

George W. Barnard M.D.

Learning to Befriend Death

*I am trying to learn a new way of relating to death
Now I have the opportunity to see how it is going
In just two days I have had two loved ones
welcomed into the arms of death*

*Why is it so hard for me
I only have to recall my experiences
I only have to remember my childhood*

*My pain with death began with
the death of my father when I was 9 years old
This traumatic loss in my childhood
marked me – wounded me*

*No – this trauma conditioned me
and oh – how well I learned*

*My brain was sensitized to abandonment –
so sensitized it only took a little stimulus –
a little taste of death – to evoke a major reaction in me*

*It did not evoke a conscious response
Instead I experienced a primitive emotional reaction
when my Amygdala – a part of my brain –
became activated by a non-conscious
abandonment memory from childhood*

*This reaction was not under my control for a long time
but there came a time when I said "I want to be different
– both in my awareness and my responses to death"
It all began with a change in my mindset*

Unlocking Life's Secrets

*I needed to respond to death not with my child brain
but with my adult brain*

*I needed to give up some false beliefs
and replace them with a new reality
I have viewed loved ones as objects that can be possessed
I now understand that they are neither objects
nor are they to be possessed*

*No matter how strong my attachment to them
I cannot control their final destiny*

*At some time we all have to surrender to death
and meet the next phase of our life's journey*

*With this mindset I was calling on my Orbital Medial
Prefrontal Cortex – a new part of my brain –
to intervene and calm the Amygdala –
so my reaction would not be so strong*

*Today as I went to the funeral of a friend
I had an opportunity to see how well it was working
I must say my reaction certainly was more subdued than
in the past and for this I am thankful*

*But there were enough emotional rumbles
to let me know that this volcano is still active
and needs to be respected*

This means I still have work to do

∞

George W. Barnard M.D.

Lessons of Life/Death

She watched her friend writhe in pain

*There was no position in which
her friend could get her body comfortable*

*The breast cancer had metastasized
to the bones in her back*

*This had come as such a shock
since her friend had been told only weeks ago that
it looked as though she had beaten the odds*

*Taking care of her friend through chemotherapy
had taken a toll on her*

*Yet she would have it no other way
That's what friends were for – wasn't it
But now seeing her friend in constant pain
was sucking her spirit –
like a vampire withdrawing blood*

*She felt so helpless – there was nothing she could do
but be present – be compassionate
be patient – and be watchful
And watchful she was*

*Not only watching her friend but also watching herself –
as she comforted – as she consoled –
her friend in her agony*

*As she watched both her friend – and herself –
she became more and more aware of
their underlying unity – their divine unity
Both were stamped – molded – in the image of God
Indeed they were divine sisters*

*This was a precious concept to her
She hung onto it – it gave her nurturance
as she trudged through many sleepless nights*

*This divine awareness was the power that began to
transform her fragmented – torn self*

*Watching her friend struggle daily
with the demons of cancer
brought her to deal with her own mortality*

*She began to use her newfound courage
to fight her own secret fears – her self-doubts
In a way she fought her own battle with death –
death of her previous self –
which had kept her prisoner for so many years*

*In the process of dying
she resurrected into a new – freer being*

*In befriending her friend
she learned how to befriend her Self*

*Ah – the lessons of life
Ah – the lessons of death
Does it really matter from which we learn*

∞

George W. Barnard M.D.

Life and Death as Process

*Most of us have grown up fearing death
We have seen death as the enemy –
the cruel one to be avoided*

*Since we have so dreaded death
we often deny its very existence*

*We say
"He passed away" rather than "He died"*

*We put her body in a casket
and apply rouge and lipstick on her face –
and even put glasses on her – as though she might see*

*We pretend even to ourselves
that there is vitality in the body*

*Then we place the rigid corpse in a watertight casket
Denying to the end that maggots cannot enter therein*

*If denial is not enough we also use avoidance
as a way of handling our fear of death*

*We become competitive with death
It becomes the enemy to be conquered*

*We take drastic – sometimes cruel – measures
in our attempt to defeat death*

But with all this we pay a price

*We become so preoccupied with being the hero
that we fail to acknowledge death
as it approaches to take us by the hand*

*We react out of fear
and fail to prepare for the journey*

*We fail to get the big picture that says
both life and death are a process*

In fact both life and death are but one process

*There is no beginning
There is no end
Only process*

*Process to be understood
Process to be experienced*

∞

George W. Barnard M.D.

Her Friend Helen

You could say she was like a sister to her

She was that and more
There are some things you can't tell a sister

But not Helen –
she could tell Helen anything and she often did
because she knew it would go no further

Helen just listened – without judgment
Never blaming – never shaming – just listening
Sometimes with a comment – other times not a word

She didn't know how much this meant to her
until Helen was gone and then the realization came

How secure she felt in Helen's presence
How much trust she had in Helen's ability
to listen and to accept

She wishes she had told Helen
just how much she meant to her –
but she didn't

Now that this is written
she thinks that somehow Helen knows

Now she can keep talking and in silence Helen listens

∞

On Dying

I am approaching the end of my life
I must find the meaning of it all

Why me – Why now

This is a dark and scary path
leading to where I do not know

Are you willing to walk the path with me
Are you willing to be part of my community –
my sangha – to comfort me when I am in pain –
to hold me when I am afraid

Will you simply be with me and listen when I am lonely

Are you willing to be my witness as I wrestle with God

Will you tolerate my frustration –
my anger – with the process

Will you allow me to be curious about what lies beyond

Will you rejoice with me
as I experience my wholeness
even as I am dying

∞

George W. Barnard M.D.

One Drop of Water

*At a time undetermined by me I will begin a journey
one that I was taught to dread
but now I look forward to without fear*

It is called the Walk of Death

*I cannot control this mysterious adventure
to the land of the unknown*

*It must be journeyed alone
but I have no fear*

*As one drop of water
I will join other drops
to become the ocean*

∞

Surrendering to Death

*Before coming to the emergency center
she had been in severe angina pain for hours*

Now we were in a whirlwind of activity

Nurses were rushing about

* – putting nasal oxygen tubes in place
  – inserting I.V. lines for fluids and medications
  – placing a nitroglycerin tab under her tongue
  – connecting cardio-pulmonary monitors
  – withdrawing blood for testing*

*Such a frantic pace and yet so orderly
Order in chaos – such a paradox
Yet an understandable paradox*

*I sat close to her head – quietly whispering in her ears
"Breathe in the oxygen deeply and slowly –
in through your nose – out through your mouth"
She followed my words – she paced her breathing*

*I watched the monitors –
which only indicated physiological chaos
But gradually that too changed*

*It was like revisiting the story of creation in Genesis
Out of chaos came order*

*The medicines were taking effect –
her pain was subsiding*

George W. Barnard M.D.

The heart was still racing –
but now with more regularity

The panic left her face
Equanimity took its place

She had successfully crossed a hurdle –
now we could talk
Now I could listen to her thoughts
"I am ready to go" she said
"What keeps you holding on" I asked
"He finds it hard to let me go
I have been holding on for him"

And she did for several more hours and then she let go –
after struggling for more than 20 years

After struggling for so long she surrendered to death –
surrendered peacefully – surrendered quietly

Now our task is also to surrender
Let us open our hearts and surrender
to the presence of the Divine Spirit
This then allows us to be aware of
the presence of her loving spirit

Once we feel her loving spirit then we can share
the many wonderful memories that we had with her
Sharing memories permits us
both to rejoice and to grieve

It is the kind way – the gentle way – to let go

∞

The Rosebud

She was so easy to love
She was so easy to be with

It has not been easy to let her go

Her death came so rapidly
Her death came so unexpectedly

There was no time for goodbyes
There was only time for feelings

Only time for memories
and – boy – did they come
like a dam had just busted

We did have time for rituals –
rituals that opened our hearts to the pain of loss

Rituals to renew love
Such simple acts – yet so powerful

Her friend carried out her ritual with precision

First a walk through the garden –
a pause at her memorial site
then leaving a single rosebud

This was the love bond
This allowed their friendship to go unbroken

And it did more

George W. Barnard M.D.

The magic of the rosebud continues
The mystery goes on

What happened to the rosebud
after her friend left it

Did it remain alone

Or did another pick it up
touch it lovingly
perhaps even smell its fragrance
and then give it to another Beloved

Ah the mysterious power of love continues

∞

Bibliography

Achterberg, Jeanne. *Lightning at the Gate: A Visionary Journey of Healing*. Boston: Shambhala, 2002.

Adams, J.L. *The Thought of Paul Tillich*. San Francisco: Harper and Row, 1985.

Ajaya, Swami. *Psychotherapy East and West: A Unifying Paradigm*. Homesdale, PA: The Himalayan International Institute of Yoga Science and Philosophy of the U.S.A., 1983.

Anantananda, Swami. *What's on My Mind? Becoming Inspired With New Perception*, South Fallsburg, NY: SYDA, 1996.

Anderson, Sherry R. and Hopkins, Patricia. *The Feminine Face of God: The Unfolding of the Sacred in Women*. New York: Bantam Books, 1991.

Arico, Carl J. *A Taste of Silence*. New York: Continuum, 1999.

Asper, Kathrin. *The Abandoned Child Within: On Losing and Regaining Self-Worth (translated by Sharon E. Rooks)*. New York: Fromm Intl., 1993.

Armstrong, Karen. *A History of God: The 4000 Year Quest of Judaism, Christianity and Islam*. New York: Alfred A. Knopf, 1993.

Armstrong, Karen. *The Case For God*. Harpswell, ME: Anchor, 2009.

Armstrong, Karen. *The Great Transformation: The Beginning of Our Religious Traditions*. New York: Alfred A. Knopf, 2006.

Armstrong, Karen. *The Spiral Staircase: My Climb Out Of Darkness*. New York: Alfred A. Knopf, 2004.

Armstrong, Karen. *Tongues of Fire: An Anthology of Religious and Poetic Experience*. New York: Viking, 1986.

Armstrong, Karen. *Twelve Steps to a Compassionate Life*. New York: Alfred A. Knopf, 2010.

Baker, Russell. *Growing Up*. New York: Plume Books, 1995.

Banks, Coleman (trans). *The Essential Rumi*. San Francisco: Harper, 1995.

Barnard, George W. *In Search of Soul: Journey Toward Wholeness*. Haverford, PA: Infinity, 2002.

Barnard, George W.; Flesher, Carol K.; Steinbook, Richard M. *The Treatment of Urinary Retention by Aversive Stimulus Cessation and Assertive Training. Behavior Research and Therapy Volume 4, Pages 232-236*. England: Pergamon, 1966.

Barnhart, Bruno. *Second Simplicity: The Inner Shape of Christianity*. New York: Paulist, 1999.

Batchelor, Stephen. *Alone With Others: An Existential Approach To Buddhism*. New York: Grove, 1983.

Beauregard, Mario. *Brain Wars: The Scientific Battle Over the Existence of the Mind and the Proof That Will Change the Way We Live Our Lives*. New York: HarperOne, 2013.

Bennett-Goleman, Tara. *Emotional Alchemy: How the Mind Can Heal the Heart*. New York: Harmony, 2001.

Benson, Herbert (with Stark, Mark). *Timeless Healing: The Power and Biology of Belief*. New York: Scribner, 1996.

Benson, Herbert and Proctor, William. *Relaxation Revolution: The Science and Genetics of Mind Body Healing*. New York: Scribner, 2011.

Blakney, Raymond. *Meister Eckhart.* New York: Harper and Brothers, 1941.

Bly, Robert. *The Kabir Book: Forty-four of the Ecstatic Poems of Kabir.* Toronto: Beacon, 1977.

Bly, Robert and Woodman, Marion. *The Maiden King: The Reunion of Masculine and Feminine.* New York: Owl, 1999.

Borg, Marcus. *Jesus: A New Vision: Spirit, Culture, and the Life of Discipleship.* New York: HarperCollins, 1987.

Borg, Marcus. *Jesus: Uncovering the Life, Teachings, and Relevance of a Religious Revolutionary.* New York: HarperCollins, 2006.

Borg, Marcus. *Meeting Jesus Again for the First Time: The Historical Jesus and the Heart of Contemporary Faith.* New York: HarperCollins, 1994.

Borg, Marcus. *The God We Never Knew: Beyond Dogmatic Religion to a More Authentic Contemporary Faith.* New York: HarperCollins, 1998.

Borg, Marcus. *The Heart of Christianity: Rediscovering a Life of Faith.* New York: HarperCollins, 2003.

Borg, Marcus, and Wright, N.T. *The Meaning of Jesus: Two Visions.* New York: HarperOne, 2007.

Borysenko, Joan. *A Woman's Journey to God: Finding the Feminine Path.* New York: Riverhead Books, 1999.

Borysenko, Joan. *Fire in the Soul.* New York: Warner, 1993.

Borysenko, Joan. *Guilt is the Teacher, Love is the Lesson.* New York: Warner Bros, 1990.

Borsenko, Joan. *The Ways of the Mystic: 7 Paths to God.* Carlsbad: Hay House, 1997.

Bourgeault, Cynthia. *Centering Prayer and Inner Awakening.* Cambridge: Cowley, 2004.

Bourgeault, Cynthia. *The Wisdom Way of Knowing: Reclaiming an Ancient Tradition to Awaken the Heart.* San Francisco: John Wiley and Son, 2003.

Brown, Daniel and Fromm, Erika. *Hypnotherapy and Hypnoanalysis.* Hillsdale, NJ: Lawrence Erlbaum, 1986.

Chidvilasananda, Swami. *My Lord Loves A Pure Heart: The Yoga of Divine Virtues,* South Fallsburg, NY: SYDA, 1994.

Chitty, John, *Dancing with Yin and Yang: Ancient Wisdom, Modern Psychotherapy and Randolph Stone's Polarity Therapy.* Boulder CO: Polarity, 2013.

Chodron, Pema. *Awakening Loving-Kindness.* Boston: Shambhala, 1996.

Chodron, Pema. *Start Where You Are: A Guide to Compassionate Living.* Boston: Shambhala, 1994.

Chodron, Pema. *The Places That Scare You: A Guide To Fearlessness in Difficult Times.* Boston: Shambhala, 2001.

Chodron, Pema. *When Things Fall Apart: Heart Advice for Difficult Times.* Boston: Shambhala, 1997.

Christ, Carol, and Plaskow, Judith. *Womanspirit Rising: A Feminist Reader in Religion.* New York: HarperCollins, 1979.

Christ, Carol P. *Diving Deep and Surfacing.* Boston: Beacon, 1995.

Christ, Carol P. *Laughter of Aphrodite: Reflections on a Journey to the Goddess.* San Francisco: Harper and Row, 1987.

Conger, John P. *Jung and Reich: The Body as Shadow.* CA: North Atlantic, 1988.

Coward, Harold. *Jung and Eastern Thought.* Albany: SUNY, 1985.

Cozolino, L.J. *The Neuroscience of Psychotherapy: Healing the Social Brain.* New York: W.W. Norton, 2010, second edition.

d'Aquili, Eugene G. and Newberg, Andrew B. *The Mystical Mind: Probing the Biology of Religious Experience.* Minneapolis: Fortress, 1999.

Dalai Lama. *Awakening the Mind, Lightening the Heart.* New York: HarperCollins, 1995.

Dalai Lama. *Kindness, Clarity and Insight.* Ithaca, NY: Lion, 1984.

Dalai Lama. *The Good Heart: A Buddhist Perspective on the Teachings of Jesus.* Boston: Wisdom, 1996.

Damasio, Antonio. *Self Comes to Mind; Constructing the Conscious Brain.* New York: Pantheon, 2010.

Davidson, Richard J (with Bagley, Sharon). *The Emotional Life of Your Brain: How Its Unique Patterns Affect the Way You Think, Feel, and Love – and How You Can Change Them.* New York: Plume, 2013.

Davidson, Richard J. and Harrington, Anne. *Visions of Compassion: Western Scientists and Tibetan Buddhists Examine Human Nature.* New York: Oxford University, 2002.

Davies, Steven L. *Jesus the Healer: Possession, Trance and the Origins of Christianity.* New York: Continuum, 1995.

Davis, John. *The Diamond Approach: An Introduction to the Teachings of A. H. Almaas.* Boston: Shambhala, 1999.

Dossey, Larry. *Space, Time and Medicine.* Boston: Shambhala, 1982.

Dourley, John P. *The Illness that We Are: A Jungian Critique of Christianity.* Toronto: Inner City Books, 1984.

Dourley, John P. *A Strategy for a Loss of Faith.* Toronto: Inner City Books, 1992.
Dourley, John P. *Love, Celibacy and the Inner Marriage.* Toronto: Inner City Books, 1987.
Dourley, John P. *The Psyche as Sacrament: A Comparative Study of C. G. Jung and Paul Tillich.* Toronto: Inner City Books, 1981.
Dreher, Diane. *The Tao of Inner Peace.* New York: HarperCollins, 1990.
Durgananda, Swami. *The Heart of Meditation: Pathways to a Deeper Experience,* South Fallsburg, NY: SYDA, 2002.
Edinger, Edward F. *Ego and Archetype.* New York: Penguin, 1972.
Edinger, Edward F. *Ego and Self: The Old Testament Prophets,* Toronto: Inner City Books, 2000.
Edinger, Edward F. *The Aion Lectures: Exploring the Self in C.G. Jung's Aion.* Toronto: Inner City Books, 1996.
Edinger, Edward F. *The Bible and the Psyche: Individuation Symbolism in the Old Testament.* Toronto: Inner City Books, 1986.
Edinger, Edward F. *The Christian Archetype: A Jungian Commentary on the Life of Christ.* Toronto: Inner City Books, 1987.
Edinger, Edward F. *The Mysterium Lectures: A Journey Through C.G. Jung's Mysterium Coniunctionis.* Toronto, Canada: Inner City Books, 1995.
Edinger, Edward F. *The Mystery of the Coniunctio: Alchemical Image of Individuation.* Toronto, Canada: Inner City Books, 1994.

Edinger, Edward F. *The Psyche in Antiquity: Book Two, Gnosticism and Early Christianity.* Toronto, Canada: Inner City Books, 1999.

Edinger, Edward F. *The Sacred Psyche: A Psychological Approach to the Psalms.* Toronto: Inner City Books, 2004.

Edinger, Edward F. *Transformation of the God Image: An Elucidation of Jung's Answer to Job.* Toronto: Inner City Books, 1992.

Easwaran, Eknath. *The End of Sorrow: The Bhagavad Gita for Daily Living, Vol. 1.* Tomales: Nilgiri, 2000.

Ellenberger, Henri F. *The Discovery of the Unconscious: The History and Evolution of Dynamic Psychiatry.* New York: Basic Books, 1970.

Enright, Robert D. *Forgiveness Is A Choice: A Step-By-Step Process for Resolving Anger and Restoring Hope.* Washington, D.C: American Psychological Association, 2001.

Epstein, Mark. *Thoughts Without A Thinker.* New York: Basic Books, 1995.

Fiorenza, Elisabeth Schussler. *In Memory of Her: A Feminist Theological Reconstruction of Christian Origin.* New York: Crossroad, 1983.

Forman, Mark D. *A Guide to Integral Psychotherapy: Complexity, Integration, and Spirituality in Practice.* Albany, NY: SUNY, 2010.

Forsyth, James. *Freud, Jung and Christianity.* Ottawa: University of Ottawa, 1989.

Fox, John. *Finding What You Didn't Lose.* New York: Tarcher/Putnam, 1997.

Fox, John. *Poetic Medicine: The Healing Art of Poem Making.* New York: Tarcher/Putnam, 1997.

Fox, Matthew. *Breakthrough: Meister Eckhart's Creation Spirituality In New Translation*. New York: Doubleday, 1980.

Fox, Matthew. *Meditations with Meister Eckhart*. Santa Fe: Bear, 1983.

Fox, Matthew. *Original Blessing*. San Francisco: Bear, 1983.

Fox, Matthew. *The Coming of the Cosmic Christ*. Scranton, PA: Harper & Row, 1988.

Frankl, Viktor E. *Man's Search for Meaning*. New York: Washington Square, 1984.

Fuller, Robert. *Alternative Medicine and American Religious Life*, New York/Oxford: Oxford University, 1989.

Fuller, Robert. *Americans and the Unconscious*. New York: Oxford University, 1986.

Gedo, John E. *Portraits of the Artist: Psychoanalysis of Creativity and Its Vicissitudes*. New York/London: Guilford, 1983.

Gilbert, Paul. *The Compassionate Mind: A New Approach to Life's Challenges*. Oakland, CA: New Harbinger, 2010.

Gimian, Carolyn Rose. *The Essential Chogyam Trungpa*. Boston: Shambhala, 1999.

Goldenberg, Naomi R. *Changing of the Gods: Feminism and the End of Traditional Religion*. Boston: Beacon, 1979.

Goldenberg, Naomi R. *Returning Words to the Flesh: Feminism, Psychoanalysis and the Resurrection of the Body*. Boston: Beacon, 1990.

Goldstein, Joseph and Kornfield, Jack. *Seeking the Heart of Wisdom: The Path of Insight Meditation*, Boston and London: Shambhala, 2001.

Goldstein, Joseph. The Experience of Insight: A Simple and Direct Guide to Buddhist Meditation. Boston: Shambhala, 1987.

Goleman, Daniel. Destructive Emotions: A Scientific Dialogue With the Dalai Lama. New York: Bantam Dell, 2003.

Goleman, Daniel. Healing Emotions: Conversations with the Dalai Lama on Mindfulness, Emotions and Health. Boston: Shambhala, 2003.

Goodman, Felicitas D. Ecstasy, Ritual and Alternate Reality: Religion in a Pluralistic World. Indiana: University, 1988.

Griffin, Day Ray. God and Religion in the Postmodern World. Albany, NY: SUNY, 1989.

Griffin, Day Ray and Smith, Huston. Primordial Truth and Postmodern Theology. Albany, NY: SUNY, 1989.

Grimes, John. A Concise Dictionary of Indian Philosophy: Sanskrit Words Defined in English. Albany: State University of New York, 1996.

Grof, Stanislav with Hal Zina Bennett The Holotropic Mind: The Three Levels of Human Consciousness and How They Shape Our Lives. San Francisco: Harper, 1990.

Groothuis, Douglas R. Unmasking the New Age. Downers Grove, Intervarsity, 1986.

Gunaratana, V. H. Mindfulness: In Plain English-Updated and Expanded Edition. Somerville, MA: Wisdom, 2002.

Gurian, Michael. Love's Journey: The Seasons and Stages of Relationship. Boston: Shambhala, 1995.

Hall, James. Hypnosis: A Jungian Perspective. New York: Guilford, 1989.

Hanh, Thich Nhat. *Living Buddha, Living Christ*. New York: Riverhead Books, 1995.
Hanh, Thich Nhat. *Taming the Tiger Within: Meditations on Transforming Difficult Emotions*. New York: Riverhead Books, 2004.
Hanh, Thich Nhat. *Teachings on Love*. Berkeley, California: Parallax, 2006.
Hannah, Barbara. *Encounters with the Soul*. Boston: Sigo, 1981.
Hanson, Rick (and Mendias, Richard). *Buddha's Brain: The Practical Neuroscience of Happiness, Love, and Wisdom*. Oakland, CA: New Harbinger, 2009.
Hayward, Jeremy W. and Varela, Francisco J. *Gentle Bridges: Conversations with the Dalai Lama on the Sciences of Mind*. Boston: Shambhala, 2001.
Helminski, Kabir E. *Living Presence: A Sufi Way to Mindfulness and the Essential Self*. New York: Jeremy P. Tarcher/Putnam, 1992.
Helminski, Kabir. *The Knowing Heart: A Sufi Path of Transformation*. Boston: Shambhala, 2000.
Hendrix, Harville. *Getting the Love You Want*. New York: Owl Books, 2001.
Hendrix, Harville. *Keeping the Love You Find*. New York: Simon & Schuster, 1993.
Hill, Daniel. *Affect Regulation Theory: A Clinical Model*. New York: W.W. Norton, 2015.
Hillman, James and Ventura, Michael. *We've Had a Hundred Years of Psychotherapy and the World's Getting Worse*. New York: HarperCollins, 1992.
Hillman, James. *The Soul's Code: In Search of Character and Calling*. New York: Warner Books, 1997.
Hoeller, Stephan A. *Jung and the Lost Gospels*. Illinois: Theosophical, 1989.

Hoeller, Stephan A. *The Gnostic Jung*. Illinois: Theosophical, 1989.

Ignatius de Loyola. *Powers of Imagining*. Albany: State University of New York, 1986.

Jacobi, Jolande. *Complex/Archetype/Symbol in the Psychology of CG Jung*. New York: Bollingen Foundation, 1974.

Jacobi, Jolande. *The Way of Individuation*. New York: Meridian, 1967.

Jacoby, Mario. *Individuation and Narcissism: The Psychology of Self in Jung and Kohut*. London and New York: Routledge, 1990.

Jacoby, Mario. *The Analytic Encounter: Transference and Human Relationship*. Toronto: Inner City Books, 1984.

Johnson, Robert A. and Ruhl, Jerry M. *Balancing Heaven and Earth*. San Francisco: HarperSanFrancisco, 1998.

Johnson, Robert A. *Ecstasy: Understanding the Psychology of Joy*. San Francisco: Harper and Row, 1987.

Johnson, Robert A. *Femininity Lost and Regained*. New York: Harper and Row, 1990.

Johnson, Robert A. *He: Understanding Masculine Psychology*. New York: Harper and Row, 1989.

Johnson, Robert A. *Inner Work*. New York: Harper Collins, 1986.

Johnson, Robert A. *Lying with the Heavenly Woman*. San Francisco: Harper, 1995.

Johnson, Robert A. *Owning Your Own Shadow*. San Francisco: HarperCollins, 1991.

Johnson, Robert A. *She: Understanding Feminine Psychology*. New York: Harper and Row, 1989.

Johnson, Robert A. *The Fisher King and the Handless Maiden.* San Francisco: HarperSanFrancisco, 1993.
Johnson, Robert A. *Transformation.* San Francisco: HarperSanFrancisco, 1991.
Johnston, William. *The Cloud of Unknowing and the Book of Privy Counseling.* New York: Doubleday, 2005.
Johnston, William. *The Inner Eye of Love: Mysticism and Religion.* London: William Collins Sons, 1978.
Johnston, William. *The Mirror Mind: Zen-Christian Dialogue.* New York: Fordham University, 1981.
Johnston, William. *The Mysticism of the Cloud of Unknowing: A Modern Interpretation.* St. Meinrad, Indiana: Abbey, 1975.
Ignatius de Loyola. *Powers of Imagining,* trans. Antonio T. de Nicolas. New York: State University of N.Y., 1986.
Kabat-Zinn, Jon. *Full Catastrophe Living.* New York: Delta Books, 1990.
Kabat-Zinn, Jon. *Wherever You Go, There You Are.* New York: Hyperion, 1994.
Kadowaki, Kakichi. *Zen and the Bible: A Priest's Experience,* trans. Joan Rieck. London: Routledge and Kegan Paul, 1980.
Kavanaugh, Kieran and Rodriquez, Otilio. *Teresa of Avila: The Interior Castle.* Mahwah, N. J. Paulist, 1979.
Kavanaugh, Kieran and Rodriquez, Otilo. *The Collected Works of Saint John of the Cross* Washington, D.C.: I.C.S., 1991.
Keating, Thomas. *Foundations for Centering Prayer and the Christian Contemplative Life.* New York: Continuum, 2004.
Keating, Thomas. *Intimacy With God: An Introduction to Centering Prayer.* New York: Crossroad, 2006.

Keating, Thomas. *Open Mind, Open Heart: The Contemplative Dimension of the Gospel.* Rockport, MA: Element Books, 1992.

Keating, Thomas. *The Spiritual Journey Series: Parts 1-5* (transcripts of 29 *The Spiritual Journey* videotapes). St. Benedict's Monastery: Snowmass, 2003.

Keen, Sam, and Fox, Anne. *Your Mythic Journey: Finding Meaning in Your Life Through Writing and Storytelling.* New York: Putnam, 1973.

Keen, Sam. *Inward Bound.* New York: Bantam Books, 1992.

Keen, Sam. *To Love and Be Loved.* New York: Bantam Books, 1997.

Kornfield, Jack and Feldman, Christina. *Soul Food.* San Francisco: Harper, 1996.

Kornfield, Jack. *A Path With Heart: A Guide through the Perils and Promises of Spiritual Life.* New York: Bantam Books, 1993.

Kriyananda, Swami. *Revelations of Christ: Proclaimed by Paramahansa Yogananda.* Nevada City, CA: Crystal Clarity, 2007.

Kurtz, Ernest, and Ketcham, K. *The Spirituality of Imperfection.* New York: Bantam Books, 1992.

Krishna, Gopi. *Kundalini: The Evolutionary Energy in Man.* Boston: Shambhala, 1970.

Ladinsky, Daniel. *The Gift: Poems by Hafiz, the Great Sufi Master.* New York: Penguin Putnam, 1999.

Ladinsky, Daniel. *The Subject Tonight is Love: 60 Wild and Sweet Poems of Hafiz.* South Carolina: Pumpkin House, 1996.

Landaw, Jonathan. *Introduction to Tantra: The Transformation of Desire*, by Lama Thubten Yeshe. Boston: Wisdom, 2001.
Le Doux, Joseph. *The Emotional Brain: The Mysterious Underpinnings of Emotional Life*. New York: Touchstone, 1998.
Lee, Jung Young. *The Theology of Change: A Christian Concept of God in an Eastern Perspective*. Maryknoll, NJ: Orbis Books, 1979.
Leonard, George and Murphy, Michael. *The Life We are Given: A Long Term Program for Realizing the Potential of Body, Mind, Heart, and Soul*. New York: Jeremy P. Tarcher/Putnam, 1995.
Lerner, Harriet. *The Dance of Anger*. New York: Harper and Row, 1985.
Levine, Peter A. *Waking the Tiger Healing Trauma: The Innate Capacity to Transform Overwhelming Experiences*. Berkeley, California: North Atlantic Books, 1997.
Levine, Stephen and Ondrea. *Embracing the Beloved: Relationship as a Path of Awakening*. New York: Anchor Books, 1996.
Levine, Stephen. *A Gradual Awakening*. New York: Anchor Books, 1979.
Levine, Stephen. *Healing Into Life and Death*. New York: Anchor Books, 1987.
Lipton, Bruce H. *The Biology of Belief: Unleashing the Power of Consciousness, Matter, & Miracles*. Carlsbad, CA: Hay House Publishers, 2008.
Lopez, Donald S. Jr. and Rockefeller, Steven C. *Christ and the Bodhisattva*. Albany, NY: State University of New York, 1987.

Lupien, Sonia. Well Stressed: Manage Stress Before It Turns Toxic. New York: Collins, 2014.
Lynn, Steven J. and Rhue, Judith W. Theories of Hypnosis: Current Models and Perspectives. London: Guilford, 1991.
Mamas, Michael. Angels, Einstein and You: A Healer's Journey. Wilsonville, OR: BookPartners, 1999.
Marion, Jim. Putting on the Mind of Christ: The Inner Work of Christian Spirituality. Charlottesville, VA. Hampton Roads, 2000.
Marion, Jim. The Death of the Mythic God: The Rise of Evolutionary Spirituality. Charlottesville, VA: Hampton Roads, 2004.
Martin, Luther H. and Goss, James. Essays on Jung and the Study of Religion. Lanham, MD: University Press of America, 1985.
McCally, Michael and Barnard, George W. Modification of the Immersion Diuresis by Hypnotic Suggestion. Psychosomatic Medicine, Volume 30, No. 3, Pages 287-297, May 1, 1968.
McLaughlin, Kathleen J. The Concept of the Mother Goddess and its Significance: The Feminine Principle from the Perspectives of Jungian Psychology, the Hindu Tantra and Christianity. Ph.D. dissertation, California Institute of Asian Studies, 1977.
Merton, Thomas. Contemplative Prayer. New York: Image, 1969.
Merton, Thomas. New Seeds of Contemplation. New York: New Directions, 2007.
Merton, Thomas. Seeds. Boston: Shambhala, 2002.
Miles, Jack. God, A Biography. New York: Alfred A. Knopf, 1995.

Miller, Alice. *The Drama of the Gifted Child*. New York: Basic Books, 1994.

Miller, Alice *Thou Shalt Not Be Aware: Society's Betrayal of the Child*. New York: New American Library, 1984.

Mitchell, Stephen. *The Gospel According to Jesus*. New York: HarperCollins, 1991.

Mitchell, Stephen. *Tao Te Ching: A New English Version*. New York: HarperCollins, 1988.

Moberg, Kerstin Uvnas and Francis, Roberta. *The Oxytocin Factor: Tapping the Hormone of Calm, Love and Healing*. Cambridge, MA: Da Capo, 2003.

Moore, Michael. *The Future of the Body: Explorations Into the Further Evolution of Human Nature*. New York: Putnam, 1992.

Moore, Robert L. *Carl Jung and Christian Spirituality*, New York: Paulist, 1988.

Moore, Robert L. and Gillette, Douglas. *King, Warrior, Magician, Lover: Rediscovering the Archetypes of the Mature Masculine*. New York: HarperCollins, 1991.

Moore, Robert L. and Meckel, Daniel J. *Jung and Christianity in Dialogue*, New York: Paulist, 1990.

Muktananda, Swami. *Play of Consciousness: A Spiritual Autobiography*, South Fallsburg, NY: SYDA, 1994.

Murphy, Michael. *The Future of the Body: Explorations Into the Further Evolution of Human Nature*. Los Angeles: Tarcher, 1992.

Naparstek, Belleruth. *Staying Well With Guided Imagery*, New York: Warner Books, 1994.

Needleman, Jacob. *Lost Christianity*. New York: Doubleday, 1980.

Newberg, Andrew B. and Waldman, Mark R. *How God Changes Your Brain: Breakthrough Findings from a Leading Neuroscientist*. New York: Ballantine Books, 2010.

Newberg, Andrew B. *Principles of Neurotheology*. Burlington, VT: Ashgate, 2010.

Nolan, Albert. *Jesus Before Christianity*. Maryknoll: Orbis Books, 1999.

O'Donohue, John. *Anam Cara: A Book of Celtic Wisdom*. New York: HarperCollins, 2004.

O'Kane, Francoise. *Sacred Chaos: Reflections on God's Shadow and the Dark Self*. Toronto: Inner City Books, 1994.

Pagels, Elaine. *Adam, Eve and the Serpent*. New York: Random House, 1988.

Pagels, Elaine. *The Gnostic Gospels*. New York: Vantage Books, 1989.

Panksepp, Jaak and Biven, Lucy. *The Archaeology of Mind: Neuroevolutionary Origins of Human Emotions*. New York: W.W. Norton, 2012.

Pearsall, Paul. *The Heart's Code: Tapping the Wisdom and Power of Our Heart Energy*. New York: Broadway Books, 1999.

Pearson, Carol S. *The Hero Within: Six Archetypes We Live By*. San Francisco: Harper, 1989.

Perry, John Weir. *The Heart of History*. Albany, New York: SUNY, 1987.

Pert, Candace B. *Everything You Need to Know to Feel Go(o)d*. Carlsbad, CA: Hay House, 2007.

Pert, Candace B. *Molecules of Emotions: The Science Behind Mind-Body Medicine*. New York: Simon & Schuster, 1999.

Pierrakos, Eva and Saly, Judith. *Creating Union: The Pathwork of Relationship.* Madison, WI: Pathwork, 1993.

Pierrakos, Eva and Thesenga, Donovan. *Fear No Evil: The Pathwork Method of Transforming the Lower Self.* Madison, WI: Pathwork, 1993.

Pierrakos, Eva and Thesenga, Donovan. *Surrender to God Within: Pathwork at the Soul Level.* Del Mar: Pathwork, 1997.

Pierrakos, Eva. *The Pathwork of Self-Transformation.* New York: Bantam Books, 1990.

Porges, S.W. *The Polyvagal Theory: Neurophysiological Foundations of Emotions, Attachment, Communication and Self-Regulation.* New York: W.W. Norton, 2011.

Rainer, Tristine. *Your Life as Story,* New York: GP Putnam's Sons, 1998.

Ray, Reginald A. *Secret of the Vajra World: The Tantric Buddhism of Tibet.* Boston: Shambhala, 2001.

Remen, Rachel Naomi. *Kitchen Table Wisdom.* New York: Riverhead Books, 1996.

Remen, Rachel Naomi. *My Grandfather's Blessings: Stories of Strength, Refuge and Belonging.* New York: Riverhead Books, 2000.

Richo, David. *How To Be an Adult in Relationships: The Five Keys to Mindful Living.* Boston: Shambhala, 2002.

Richo, David. *Shadow Dance: Liberating the Power and Creativity of Your Dark Side.* Boston: Shambhala, 1999.

Rinpoche, Yongey Mingyur and Swanson, Eric. *The Joy of Living: Unlocking the Secret and Science of Happiness.* New York: Harmony Books, 2007.

Rohr, Richard. *Everything Belongs: The Gift of Contemplative Prayer.* New York: Crossroad, 1999.

Rohr, Richard (with John Bookser Feister). *Jesus' Plan for a New World*. Cincinnati: St. Anthony Messenger, 1996.
Rollins, Wayne G. *Jung and the Bible*. Atlanta: John Knox, 1983.
Rollins, Wayne G. *The Gospels: Portrait of Christ*. Louisville, KY: Westminster, 1963.
Rosen, David. *The Tao of Jung*. New York: Penguin Books, 1996.
Rossi, Ernest L. *Psychobiology of Mind-Body Healing*. New York: Norton, 1993.
Rossi, Ernest L. *The Psychobiology of Gene Expression: Neuroscience and Neurogenesis in Hypnosis and the Healing Arts*, New York: W.W. Norton, 2002.
Ruether, Rosemary R. *Sexism and God Talk: Toward a Feminist Theology*. Boston: Beacon, 1993.
Ruether, Rosemary R. *Woman Guides: Readings Toward a Feminist Theology*. Boston: Beacon, 1985.
Sanders, Shirley. *Clinical Self Hypnosis*. New York: Guilford, 1991.
Sanford, John A. *Between People: Communicating One to One*. New York: Paulist, 1982.
Sanford, John A. *Dreams, God's Forgotten Language*. Philadelphia and New York: J.B. Lippincott, 1968.
Sanford, John A. *Evil: The Shadow Side of Reality*. New York: Crossroad, 1981.
Sanford, John A. *Fritz Kunkel: Selected Writings*. New York: Paulist, 1984.
Sanford, John A. *Healing and Wholeness*. New York: Paulist, 1977.
Sanford, John, A. *Healing Body and Soul*, Louisville, Kentucky: Westminster/John Knox Press, 1992.
Sanford, John A. *The Kingdom Within*. New York: Harper & Row, 1987.

Sanford, John A. *The Invisible Partners*. New York: Paulist, 1980.
Sanford, John A. *The Strange Trial of Mr. Hyde*. San Francisco: Harper & Row, 1987.
Schaer, Hans. *Religion and the Cure of Souls in Jung's Psychology*, New York: Pantheon Books, 1950.
Schwartz, Jeffrey, and Begley, Sharon. *The Mind and the Brain: Neuroplasticity and the Power of Mental Force.* New York: Harper Perennial, 2003.
Schwartz-Salant, Nathan. *Narcissism and Character Transformation: The Psychology of Narcissistic Character Disorders*. Toronto: Inner City Books, 1982.
Scroggs, Robin. *Christology in Paul and John: The Reality and Revelation of God*. Philadelphia: Fortress, 1988.
Segal, R. A., Singer, J. and Stein, M. *The Allure of Gnosticism: The Gnostic Experience in Jungian Psychology and Contemporary Culture*. Illinois: Open Court, 1995.
Sen Sharma, Debabrata. *The Philosophy of Sadhana*. Albany, NY: The State University of New York, 1990.
Siegel, Daniel S. *The Mindful Brain: Reflection and Attunement in the Cultivation of Well-Being*. New York: W.W. Norton, 2007.
Sinetar, Marsha. *Ordinary People As Monks and Mystics: Lifestyles for Self-discovery*. New York: Paulist, 1986.
Singer, June. *Boundaries of the Soul - The Practice of Jung's Psychology*. New York: Doubleday, 1994.
Singer, June. *Energies of Love: Sexuality Revisited*. New York: Anchor, 1983.

Singer, June. *Seeing Through the Visible World: Jung, Gnosis and Chaos.* San Francisco: Harper & Row, 1990.
Smedes, Lewis B. *Forgive and Forget: Healing the Hurts We Don't Deserve.* New York: Simon & Schuster, 1984.
Smedes, Lewis B. *Shame and Grace – Healing the Shame We Don't Deserve.* New York: HarperCollins, 1993.
Smedes, Lewis B. *The Art of Forgiving: When You Need to Forgive and Don't Know How.* New York: Ballantine Books, 1996.
Smith, Curtis D. *Jung's Quest for Wholeness: A Religious and Historical Perspective.* Albany, NY: State University of New York, 1990.
Smith, C. Michael. *Jung and Shamanism in Dialogue: Retrieving the Soul/Retrieving the Sacred.* Mahwah: Paulist, 1997.
Smith, Huston. *Forgotten Truth: The Common Vision of the World's Religions.* New York: HarperCollins, 1992.
Smith, Huston. *The World's Religions.* New York: HarperCollins, 1991.
Smoley, Richard. *Inner Christianity: A Guide to the Esoteric Tradition.* Boston: Shambhala, 2002.
Spong, John Shelby. *Living in Sin: A Bishop Rethinks Human Sexuality.* New York: HarperCollins, 1988.
Spong, John Shelby. *Why Christianity Must Change or Die.* San Francisco: HarperSan Francisco, 1998.
Stein, Murray. *Jung's Map of the Soul: An Introduction.* Chicago: Open Court, 1998.
Stein, Murray. *Jung's Treatment of Christianity: The Psychotherapy of a Religious Tradition.* Wilmette, IL: Chiron, 1985.
Stein, Murray and Moore, Robert L. *Jung's Challenge to Contemporary Religion.* Wilmette, IL: Chiron, 1987.

Stettbacher, J. Konrad. *Making Sense of Suffering: The Healing Confrontation with Your Own Past.* New York: Dutton, 1991.

Stevens, Anthony. *The Two Million -Year Old Self.* College Station: Texas A&M University, 1993.

Suzuki, D. T. *An Introduction to Zen Buddhism.* New York: Grove, 1964.

Sviri, Sara. *The Taste of Hidden Things: Images on the Sufi Path.* Inverness, CA: The Golden Sufi Center, 2002.

Thesenga, Susan. *The Undefended Self: Living the Pathwork.* Madison: Pathwork, 2001.

Tolle, Eckhart. *A New Earth: Awakening to Your Life's Purpose.* New York: Penguin Group, 2006.

Tolle, Eckhart. *The Power of Now.* Novato: New World Library, 1999.

Trible, Phyllis. *God and the Rhetoric of Sexuality.* Philadelphia: Fortress, 1978.

Trungpa, Chogyam. *Cutting Through Spiritual Materialism.* Boston: Shambhala, 1973.

Trungpa, Chogyam. *Meditation in Action.* Berkeley, CA: Shambala, 1969.

Trungpa, Chogyam. *Shambhala - The Sacred Path of the Warrior.* Boston: Shambhala, 1988.

Tulku, Tarthang. *Openness Mind.* Berkeley, CA: Dharma, 1978.

Tweedie, Irina. *The Chasm of Fire: A Woman's Experience of Liberation through the Teachings of a Sufi Master.* Worcester, England. Element Books, 1979.

Ulanov, Ann Belford. *Religion and the Spiritual in Carl Jung.* New York: Paulist, 2000.

Ulanov, Ann and Barry. *Religion and the Unconscious.* Philadelphia: Westminster, 1975.

Ulanov, Ann and Barry. *Healing Imagination*. Daimon Verlag, 1999.
Vaillant, George. *Spiritual Evolution: A Scientific Defense of Faith*. New York: Broadway Books, 2008.
Vaillant, Leigh McCullough. *Changing Character: Short Term Anxiety-Regulating Psychotherapy for Restructuring Defenses, Affects and Attachment*. New York: Basic Books, 1997.
Vaughan, Frances. *Shadows of the Sacred*. Wheaton, IL: Quest Books, 1995.
Von Franz, Marie Louise. *Alchemical Active Imagination*. Boston: Shambhala, 1997.
Von Franz, Marie-Louise. *Shadow and Evil in Fairy Tales*. Dallas: Spring, 1974.
Walker, Alice. *Banished Knowledge – Facing Childhood Injuries*. New York: Nan A. Talese/Doubleday, 1990.
Walker, Alice. *Drama of the Gifted Child: The Search for the True Self*. New York: Basic Books, 1994.
Walker, Alice. *Thou Shalt Not Be Aware: Society's Betrayal of the Child*. New York: New American Library, 1984.
Wallace, B. Alan (with Wilhelm, Steven). *Tibetan Buddhism From the Ground Up: A Practical Approach for Modern Life*. Boston: Wisdom, 1993.
Wallace, B. Alan. *Choosing Reality: A Buddhist View of Physics and the Mind*. Ithaca: Snow Lions, 1996.
Walsh, Roger N. *Essential Spirituality*. New York: John Wiley and Sons, 1999.
Walsh, Roger N. *The Spirit of Shamanism*. New York: Tarcher/Putnam, 1990.
Washburn, Michael. *The Ego and the Dynamic Ground: A Transpersonal Theory of Human Development*. Albany, NY: State University of New York, 1995.

Watts, Alan. *Myth and Ritual in Christianity.* Boston: Beacon, 1968.

Watts, Alan. *This Is It.* New York: Pantheon Books, 1960.

Welwood, John. *Awakening the Heart: East/West Approaches to Psychotherapy and the Healing Relationship.* Boston: Shambhala, 1985.

Welwood, John. *Challenge of the Heart: Love, Sex and Intimacy in Changing Times.* Boston: Shambhala, 1985.

Welwood, John. *Journey of the Heart: The Path of Conscious Love.* New York: HarperCollins, 1996.

Wilber, Ken. *The Eye of the Spirit: An Integral Vision for a World Gone Slightly Mad.* Boston: Shambhala, 2001.

Welwood, John. *The Meeting of the Ways: Explorations in East/West Psychology.* New York: Schocken Books, 1979.

Welwood, John. *Toward a Psychology of Awakening: Buddhism, Psychotherapy, and the Path of Personal and Spiritual Transformation.* Boston: Shambhala, 2000.

Wilber, Ken. *A Brief History of Everything.* Boston: Shambhala, 2007.

Wilbur, Ken. *Grace and Grit: Spirituality and Healing in the Life and Death of Treya Killam Wilber.* Boston: Shambhala, 2000.

Wilber, Ken. *Integral Psychology: Consciousness, Spirit, Psychology, Therapy.* Boston. Shambhala, 2000.

Wilbur, Ken. *Integral Spirituality: A Startling New Role for Religion in the Modern and Postmodern World.* Boston: Shambhala, 2006.

Wilber, Ken. *One Taste: Daily Reflections on Integral Spirituality.* Boston. Shambhala, 2000.

Wilber, Ken. *Sex, Ecology, Spirituality: The Spirit of Evolution.* Boston. Shambhala Publications, 2000.

Wilbur, Ken. *The Atman Project*. Wheaton, IL: Theosophical, 1996.

Wilber, Ken. *The Marriage of Sense and Soul: Integrating Science and Religion*. New York: Random House, 2011.

Wilbur, Ken. *The Spectrum of Consciousness*. Wheaton, IL: Quest Books, 1993.

Wilber, Ken. *Up From Eden: A Transpersonal View of Human Evolution*. Boston: Shambhala, 1981.

Wilcox, Brian K. *An Ache for Union: Poems on Oneness with God through Love*. Bloomington, IN: First Books, 2003.

Williamson, Marianne. *A Return to Love: Reflections on the Principles of A Course in Miracles*. New York: HarperCollins, 1993.

Wink, Walter. *The Powers That Be: Theology for a New Millennium*. New York: Doubleday, 1998.

Wolf, Fred Alan. *The Spiritual Universe*. New York: Simon & Schuster, 1996.

Woodman, Marion and Dickson, Elinor. *Dancing in the Flames*. Boston: Shambhala, 1996.

Wren, Brian. *What Language Shall I Borrow: God Talk in Worship: A Male Response to Feminist Theology*. New York: Crossroad, 1991.

Zukav, Gary. *The Seat of the Soul*. New York: Simon and Schuster, 1989.

Zweig, Connie and Abrams. *Meeting the Shadow: The Hidden Power of the Dark Side of Human Nature*. New York: Penguin Putnam, 1991.

Index of Poems

A Model of Love, 319
A Secret No More, 49
A Stranger No More, 318
Accepting Nurturance from the Soul, 323
Approaching Retirement, 76
Attunement, 276
Becoming Aware of Love, 327
Becoming We-centric, 21
Being Human, 183
Birthing the Stone, 55
Bonding Behavior, 239
Changing My Response to Criticism, 13
Chit-Sat-Ananda/Awareness-Being-Bliss, 155
Complicated Families, 280
Connection to the Primal, 79
Conquering Fear, 110
Coping with Stress, 251
Dealing with My Mortality, 343
Early Traumatic Relationships Impact Us, 282
Emerging from an Act of Betrayal, 43
Encountering the Divine, 28
Encouraging Him On, 57
Endorphin Bursting Into Glee, 313
Enjoying the Joy, 321
Entering My Sacred Space, 95
essence is Essence, 158
Evolutionary Brain, 199
Expanding My Boundaries, 54
Experiencing Being, 59
Experiencing My Essential Nature, 4
Experiencing the Freshness of My Being, 18
Experiencing the Numinous, 70

Experiencing the Power of the Amygdala, 224
Facing a Big Decision, 285
Facing Death Without Fear, 344
Fears from Childhood, 322
Feast at the Master's Table, 159
Finding a Safe Haven, 60
Finding God/dess Within, 30
Finding Harmony in the Numinous, 161
Finding the One, 169
Forgiveness is Mine, 98
Gaining Access to Healing Memories, 100
Genuine Concern for the Other, 19
Gestation of the Love Child, 340
Getting Closure through Acceptance, 288
Getting in Harmony with the Eternal, 222
Getting Through to God, 163
Giving Up My Blindness, 164
God Needs Me, 165
Goodbye Dear Friend, 346
Goodbye Friend - Hello Angel, 352
Gratitude, 339
Harnessing Primal Energies, 33
Having Self-Compassion, 63
Her Friend Helen, 359
Him and His Old Dog, 290
Homecoming, 152
How Memories Influence Us, 324
How Our BodyMindSpirit Communicates, 210
Humans Become Social Beings, 204
Hungry for the Beloved, 328
I – As Co-Creator, 166
I Ask Your Forgiveness, 103
I Knew Him So Well, 347
In My Footsteps, 314
Inner Resources, 6

Inner Transformation, 81
Inward Bound, 66
Journey Called Mourning, 351
Journey of Change, 71
Joyful Reunion, 167
Judgmental Self, 8
Kundalini, 73
Laboring to Bring Forth a New Creation, 292
Learning Self-Regulation, 235
Learning to Befriend Death, 353
Learning to Let Go of Chronic Stress, 260
Lessons of Life/Death, 355
Let Us Open Our Hearts, 329
Letting Be, 7
Letting Go, 294
Letting Go of Old Tapes, 104
Liberation from Resentment and Hatred, 36
Life and Death as Process, 357
Life Sparks, 168
Lifting the Veil from Childhood Emotions, 88
Longing for a Life that Matters, 126
Loosen My Bond, 179
Lovers Loving, 40
Maitri, 106
Mammy, 297
Many Faceted Self, 1
Member of the Club, 246
Midwife – Guide – Mentor, 298
Miracles Still Happen, 108
Moments to Cherish, 300
Motion of the Butterfly, 170
Moving On, 93
My Heart Grew Hands, 109
My Spiritual Gourd, 114
Mythic Journey, 82

Now I am the Gardener, 301
Old and New Responses to Threat, 192
On Dying, 360
One Drop of Water, 361
One Integrated Brain, 187
Our Home is Special, 303
Path to Freedom, 74
Perils of the Danger-O-Stat, 217
Post-traumatic Stress Disorder (PTSD), 272
Preventing an Emotional Meltdown, 264
Prisoner in My Own Being, 86
Realizing God's Presence, 171
Receiving the Bouquet, 307
Reclaiming My Wholeness, 17
Reply from the Thou, 116
Say Hello to God, 175
Secrets of the Brain, 195
Seeking an Anchor, 51
Seeking and Receiving Blessings, 308
Seeking the Watering Hole, 120
Sharing Life's Breath, 80
She Still Has the Memory, 330
Spirit Waiting for Me, 176
Spring Ecstasy, 309
Standing on the Shoulders, 311
Stress Burnout, 267
Suffering is Part of Isness, 122
Surrendering to Death, 362
Sweet Words Lingered On, 350
Sympathetic Nervous System Overload, 269
The Aftermath of Death, 348
The Aftermath of Sexual Assault, 137
The Dynamics of Stress, 254
The Empty Vessel that is Full, 177
The Final Letting Go, 342

The Inner Crucible, 124
The Origins of Love, 333
The Overstressed Mom, 242
The Perfect Hostess, 117
The Power of Compassion, 331
The Power of the Heart, 338
The Re-Awakening, 128
The Rosebud, 364
The Wonders of Oxytocin, 229
Tis a Gift, 48
True Identity, 178
Two Basic Needs, 337
Unfolding From Being, 143
Unfolding into Wholeness, 317
Unlocking One of Life's Secrets, 232
Unnamed Woman, 144
Walking from the Cave of Darkness, 78
Watching the Mind, 3
Welcome Home My Son, 304
Who Benefits from Forgiveness, 150
With Forgiveness Comes Relief, 153
With Spirits Renewed, 180
You Are Accepted, 147
You Are Not Alone, 181